ato
bodysl

M000033354
to
whiskey
zippers

Atomic Bodyslams to Whiskey Zippers

Cocktails

for the

21st Century

ADAM ROCKE

Surrey Books
Chicago

For my grandparents,
Alice and Julius, Mary and Sande,
for always being there—
whether in person or in spirit.

ATOMIC BODYSLAMS TO WHISKEY ZIPPERS: COCKTAILS FOR THE 21ST CENTURY is published by Surrey Books, Inc. 230 E. Ohio St., Suite 120, Chicago, IL 60611

Copyright©1997 by Adam Rocke
All rights reserved, including the right to reproduce this book or portions thereof in any form, including any information storage or retrieval system, except for the inclusion of brief quotations in a review.

First edition: 3 4 5
This book is manufactured in the United States of America

Library of Congress Cataloging-in-Publication data:

Rocke, Adam.
  Atomic bodyslams to whiskey zippers: cocktails
for the 21st century / Adam Rocke.
     p. cm.
  Includes index.
  ISBN 1-57284-101-2
1. Cocktails. I. Title
TX951.R63 1997
641.8'74—dc21   97-969
                                   CIP

Editorial and production: Bookcrafters, Inc., Chicago
Design and typesetting: Joan Sommers Design, Chicago

For free book catalog and prices on quantity purchases, contact Surrey Books at the address above.

Distributed to the trade by Publishers Group West.

ACKNOWLEDGMENTS

Atomic Bodyslams to Whiskey Zippers was an absolute joy to write. It brought back many memories of my drink experimentation days. Fortunately, I was usually not the one doing the initial tasting—I gave away a lot of free drinks in the process. So, to all my tasters, official and unofficial, I thank you from the bottom of my heart (and stomach).

Also, I'd be remiss without extending my sincerest thanks to Susan Schwartz and the rest of the gang at Surrey Books. And to my editor, Gene DeRoin, who waded through my many misspellings and grammatical errors, probably wondering if I was soused when I typed the manuscript. Thank you for all your hard work.

Finally, to my parents, Robin and Richard, my sister, Kim, and my brother, Sande. This round's on me!

13
ONE/THE BASICS

THE SET-UP: UTENSILS, GLASSES,
MEASUREMENTS & SIZES, MIXES & GARNISHES,
LIQUOR GLOSSARY, HELPFUL HINTS.

25
TWO/THE USUAL SUSPECTS

ALL OF THE OLD STANDBYS AND TRADITIONAL
FAVORITES/MANY WITH A NEW, 21ST CENTURY
TWIST.

53
THREE/LOW-TOXICITY FUN & PARTY DRINKS

BEST-TASTING DRINKS THAT SHOULDN'T LEAVE
YOU GOOGLY-EYED AND STUMBLING.

90
FOUR/SLAM 'EM AND GET HAMMERED

TRY THESE LITTLE JAMMERS IF
YOUR GOAL IS TO GET BOMBED.

108

FIVE/I DRANK WHAT?

UNHOLY CONCOCTIONS THAT A SOBER PERSON
PROBABLY WOULD NOT ORDER.

132

SIX/I DON'T WANNA REMEMBER A THING!

ELIXIRS THAT WILL MAKE YOU FORGET
ANYTHING YOU DID THE NIGHT BEFORE.

156

SEVEN/YOU DON'T EXPECT ME TO DRINK THAT, DO YOU?

SOME OF THESE "HOMEGROWN" POTIONS
ARE REALLY GOOD—BUT GETTING PAST
THE NAME IS TOUGH.

175

EIGHT/HOT DRINKS FOR COLD BODIES

HOT, TASTY BEVERAGES—WITH A
HEALTHY DOSE OF ALCOHOL—TO TAKE
THE STING OUT OF YOUR DAY.

The bar business is thriving! It seems that everybody wants a drink these days—and who could blame them? I'd be willing to bet that most of us—at one time or another—would prefer to escape reality courtesy of a mind-boggling concoction than deal with the druthers and grind of everyday life.

However, in today's scheme of high-tech mixology and trend-setting "fashion" drinks, ordinary elixirs like Gin and Tonic, Vodka Martinis, and Bloody Marys just don't cut it. In fact, they don't even come close. Today, everybody wants a change. Image is *everything!* (At least, that's what all the ads say.)

But what are you going to have? You can't just throw ice in a glass and pour in the first things you grab—though that does happen quite frequently, with results oftentimes less than desirable. So what's the answer?

Quite frankly, the answer is simple. But let me caution you now: this is *not* your father's bar manual. This is not a list of many funky ingredients thrown together in some pour-and-hope manner, and this is certainly not "Mr. Boston's."

No, these are *Cocktails for the 21st Century*, where drinks like the Atomic Bodyslam, Squashed Frog, PMS Special, Mind Eraser, Chocolate Zorro, and (one of my personal favorites) Horny Monkey rule the night.

On the following pages you will find recipes for the newest, the wildest, and the most outlandish drinks being served in today's trendiest bars and nightclubs.

Trust me on this one. I know As a struggling actor in the City of Broken Dreams I spent three to four nights a week mixing and pouring these godforsaken potions. Night after night, it amazed me to see what some people put into their bodies. I just don't know how they do it. And while it's true that many of these recipes are actually quite potable and, yes, even tasty, a good number of the others should probably be registered with the Poison Control Center of America. Especially some of the ones I created. (That's what bartenders do when business is slow.) Still, somebody had to make the drinks and, in between my gigs, that somebody was me.

So here she is—the mother of all drink guides. Perfect for the professional and amateur alike. No true bartender should be without it. Whether for your business or your home, you're guaranteed to find a drink to fit the occasion. After all, if you can imagine it, it's probably in here.

But before you read on, let me just take the opportunity to thank my many tasters—and there were *many* —who, for the wondrous joy of a (all bar owners look away!) free drink, received first-dibs on some of my creations. For those of you who didn't particularly enjoy the experience, let me just say I'm sorry but, hell, I warned you. Besides, wasn't I the one who called the ambulance? Seriously, thanks again. This book's for you.

Whether it's your home bar or a professional saloon, the initial "set-up" is probably the most important thing. Sure, you can add to it as you go, but starting off right is starting off best. Here's how:

UTENSILS

As with any hobby or profession, there are millions of little gizmos and gadgets on the market one can purchase to use for a multitude of purposes. The arena of mixology is no different. But instead of maxing out your credit cards on every tool and utensil under the sun, here's a list of the items you'll use most often when you're behind the bar.

BLENDER (newer versions with multiple speeds are the best)

CAN and **BOTTLE OPENERS**

COCKTAIL SHAKER

CORKSCREW (the new air-powered "pump" varieties are excellent)

CUTTING BOARD (wooden or synthetic)

ICE BUCKET (it doesn't hurt to have a **CHAMPAGNE BUCKET** too)

ICE CREAM SCOOPER

ICE TONGS

JUICER (more pompously known as a **JUICE EXTRACTOR**)

KNIVES (any small set; make sure a **PARING KNIFE** is included)

LEMON/LIME SQUEEZER

MEASURING SET (includes various-sized cups and spoons)

MIXING BOWLS (preferably two small and one large)

MIXING GLASS

MIXING STICK (also known as a **MUDDLER**; usually wooden)

NAPKINS (cocktail and, for goblet-sized drinks, dinner)

PITCHERS (for measuring and/or serving)

PLASTIC STRAWS (cocktail and long)

PUNCH BOWL SET (with at least six glasses)

SALT & PEPPER SHAKERS

SAUCERS (for holding salt and sugar while you frost glasses)

SHAKER SET (consisting of a metal tumbler and a mixing glass)

SPOONS (Teaspoons and Tablespoons, if not in Measuring Set)

STRAINER (two: medium and very fine mesh)

SWIZZLE STICKS

TOOTHPICKS (for garnishes)

TOWELS or **RAGS** (for cleaning purposes)

As stated previously, there are many other "odds and ends." Personal taste (and funds) will dictate exactly what you buy. For example: colorful, shaped toothpicks are much nicer than plain wooden ones, as are colored, or logo-imprinted cocktail napkins as compared to plain white. The choice is yours.

GLASSES

Now that your "accessory drawer" is full, it's time to think about what you'll be serving your concoctions in. The following is a list of what's out there. Again, exactly what you need and the style you choose is up to you.

BALLOON These are large wine glasses in the 8- to 14-ounce range.

BEER MUG Ranging anywhere from 12 to 16 ounces and as much as 22 ounces for the over-sized varieties.

CHAMPAGNE FLUTE For champagne, Bellinis, and other champagne and wine drinks. Ranging from 4 to 8 ounces.

CHAMPAGNE SAUCER For wine or champagne. Usually about 4 ounces.

CHAMPAGNE TULIP Ranges from 4 to 6 ounces.

COCKTAIL There are a wide variety of cocktail glasses on the market, ranging anywhere from 3 to 6 ounces with varying sizes in between (such as $3 \frac{1}{2}$, $4 \frac{1}{2}$, $4 \frac{3}{4}$, etc.). Again, personal taste will dictate, but, if possible, it's always nice to have two sizes (at least) on hand.

COLLINS Multiple-ingredient drinks are usually served in Collins glasses, as are many "juice" and "cola" drinks. They range from 10 to about 14 ounces, and there are some, called **TALL COLLINS**, which can be as large as 16 ounces.

CORDIAL (also called **PONY**) Never more than 2 ounces, this small glass is most commonly used for after-dinner liqueurs, brandys, cordials, and layered shots.

DOUBLE ROCKS (also called **DOUBLES**) For "rocks" drinks, these range from 12 to 16 ounces.

GOBLET Again, there are a wide variety of goblets. Beer goblets are traditionally 12 ounces, whereas other types can range from 10 to 14 ounces.

HIGHBALL A very common glass, these range from 8 to 12 ounces.

HOT MUG Avoid using glass for the hot drinks (unless you're serving tea to a Russian). These mugs, ranging from 10 to 12 ounces, up to 16 ounces for the oversized varieties, are used for all the hot chocolate and hot coffee drinks. Ciders and teas can also be served in a Hot Mug.

HURRICANE GLASS Excellent for two-person exotic drinks, this huge goblet is usually 22 ounces. However, I have seen some in "Island" bars that were as big as 30 ounces.

JIGGER (see **SHOT GLASSES**)

MARTINI These V-shaped glasses, usually in the 4- to 5-ounce range, are perhaps the most famous of the lot.

MUG (see **BEER MUG** and **HOT MUG**)

OLD FASHIONED (also called **LOWBALL** or **ROCKS**) Very common glasses in the 6- to 8-ounce range. **BIG OLD FASHIONED** holds 2 to 4 ounces more.

PARFAIT A tall, somewhat narrow glass ranging from 7 to 8 ounces.

PILSNER A variety of beer glass in the 10- to 16-ounce range.

POUSSE-CAFÉ From 2 to 4 ounces, these glasses are the larger version of the Cordial/Pony glasses.

SHERRY These can range anywhere from 3 to 4 ounces.

SHOT GLASSES Another type of glass with many size variations. I have seen them as small as $1/2$ ounce and some as large as 3 ounces (called **MONSTER SHOTS**). Another shot glass, the **JIGGER**, is traditionally $1^1/2$ ounces.

SNIFTER An elegant, gently curved glass for serving cognac and brandy, these come in a wide array of sizes from 3 to 14 ounces. Traditionally, 6 ounces is the norm.

SOUR (also called **WHISKEY SOUR** or **DELMONICO** or **GO-GO**) While it can be used for a wide array of drinks, it most commonly houses sours. They range from 5 to 6 ounces.

WINE Look for a virtually endless variety of shapes and sizes in this category, ranging from 5 to 12 ounces, though I'm sure there are smaller and larger ones available. And while most people use the same glasses for white or red wine, red wine glasses are traditionally more rounded for "bouquet" purposes.

YARD (also called **ENGLISH YARD**) While the true definition of a yard is 3 feet, or 36 inches, some stateside bars offer beer or ale in Yard glasses. The ones that I have seen were smaller variations, called **HALF-YARDS**. They usually come in a wooden holder. Yards can hold anywhere from 30 to 48 ounces.

BAR MEASUREMENTS

The following equivalent measurements are a must for all bartenders, amateurs, and professionals alike:

1 cup	8 ounces
1 split	6.4 ounces
1 wineglass	4 ounces
1 jigger	1 1/2 ounces
1 pony	1 ounce
1 tablespoon (tbsp.)	3/8 ounce
1 teaspoon (tsp.)	1/8 ounce
1 dash	1/32 ounce

BOTTLE SIZES OF WINES & SPIRITS

TYPE	SIZE FL. OZ.	SIZE METRIC
gallon	128.0	3.5 L
double magnum	101.4	3.0 L
half gallon	64.0	1.75 L
magnum	50.7	1.5 L
quart	32.0	1.0 L
fifth	25.6	750 ML
pint	16.0	500 ML
tenth	12.8	375 ML
half pint	8.0	200 ML
split	6.4	187 ML
minature	1.6	50 ML

MIXERS, GARNISHES & "EXTRAS"

Once again, stocking your bar is a matter of personal taste. Here's a list of suggested items:

BITTERS The two most popular varieties are orange and Angostura.

BLOODY MARY MIX Many varieties on the market. In most cases, all you need to add is vodka (or other alcohol) and garnish.

CHERRIES We're talking **maraschino** here. Two colors are available: green and red.

CINNAMON STICKS Can be used as stirrers in cold or hot drinks.

CLUB SODA

COFFEE

COLA

CREAM Light and heavy.

CREAM OF COCONUT

EGGS Make sure they're fresh.

FALERNUM This spicy sweetener can be used in a variety of drinks.

GINGER ALE

GRENADINE Made from pomegranates, this sweet, colorful (red) flavoring will see a lot of use.

ICE Cubes, cracked, and crushed; some bars keep a block of ice and actually "shave" it for certain drinks. It's a nice touch if you have the time.

ICE CREAM & SHERBET Flavors are your choice.

JUICES Apple, cranberry, grapefruit, lemon, lime, orange, passion fruit, pineapple, prune, and tomato. Other "exotic" juices and nectars (kiwi, star fruit, mango, etc.) are available.

LEMONS You'll need wedges and slices, not to mention twists from the rinds.

LIMES Used exactly as you would lemons.

MAPLE SYRUP

MILK

MINT LEAVES Used in some "tea" drinks and Juleps.

NUTMEG This seed of an East Indian tree is grated and used to spice (or dust) certain hot chocolate/coffee drinks and Brandy Alexanders.

OLIVES It's best to use those *without* pits, such as the green variety, which are commonly found in Martinis.

ONIONS These are the tiny ones called **PEARL** onions. They come pickled.

ORANGES Use slices, thick chunks (mashed), or the rinds for making orange twists.

ORGEAT Very simply, **ALMOND SYRUP.**

PEPPER Black is the most common, but you might choose to keep red on hand, as well.

PIÑA COLADA MIX Has all the essential ingredients except the rum.

PINEAPPLES Chunks, slices, and, for "Island"-style drinks, long spears.

ROSE'S LIME JUICE Differs from fresh lime juice because it contains a sugar-based syrup.

SALT

SELTZER

SOUR MIX

SPRITE or 7-UP

SUGAR White granulated sugar and brown sugar are used most often.

TABASCO SAUCE A spicy red sauce used in Bloody Marys and other drinks. They now have a green version made with extra-hot jalapeño peppers.

TONIC WATER (also called **QUININE**)

WATER Distilled, sparkling, or spring. If possible, try to avoid using tap water in drinks. Your guests/ customers will appreciate it.

WORCESTERSHIRE SAUCE A spicy sauce made with soy sauce, vinegar, and spices. It makes a great addition to Bloody Marys and other drinks.

LIQUOR GLOSSARY

Okay, you've got all the gadgets you need, you've got your glasses memorized, and you've got your garnishes and mixers laid out for easy use. Now, all you need to know, besides the recipes, of course, is the differences among the various liquors and liqueurs. Here they are:

ABISANTE Pale green liqueur similar in flavor to anisette (licorice).

ADVOKAAT Eggnog-flavored liqueur.

ALE Bitter-tasting lager.

AMARETTO Almond-flavored liqueur.

AMER PICON A French combination of quinine, gentian, and oranges.

ANISETTE Also called **ANISE**; licorice-flavored liqueur.

ARMAGNAC Similar to cognac but only distilled once.

BAILEY'S Irish cream liqueur.

BANANA LIQUEUR Also called **CRÈME DE BANANA.**

BENEDICTINE A liqueur made by the French Benedictine monks.

BLACKBERRY LIQUEUR Like other "fruit" liqueurs, this cordial has the distinct flavor of its namesake.

BLENDED WHISKEY Different whiskeys combined (called "married") in the casks.

BOURBON WHISKEY Aged for at least two years in white oak casks and made mainly from corn.

BRANDY Basically, the fermented juice of fruit. Comes in many varieties: cherry, blackberry, apricot, etc.

CANADIAN WHISKEY Made from rye, barley, and corn.

CHAMBORD A French liqueur with a very distinct sweet raspberry taste.

CHAMBRAISE Another sweet French liqueur, this one is made from wild strawberries.

CHARTREUSE Two types, yellow and green, created in France by Carthusian monks.

CHERRY HEERING A cherry-flavored liqueur.

COGNAC Fine brandy from France's Cognac region.

COINTREAU Orange-flavored liqueur made from curaçao oranges.

CRÈME LIQUEURS Many flavors, such as **CRÈME DE CACAO** (light and dark), **CRÈME DE MENTHE** (white and green), **CRÈME DE CASSIS**, and others, all with a creamy consistency and sweet taste.

CURAÇAO Orange-flavored liqueur that can be blue or orange.

DRAMBUIE A malt whiskey-based liqueur with a relatively sweet taste.

DUBONNET A sweet-spicy French aperitif.

FRAISES Strawberry-flavored liqueur.

FRAMBOISE Another raspberry-flavored liqueur.

FRANGELICO Italian hazelnut-flavored liqueur.

GALLIANO Yellow-gold Italian liqueur made from various herbs and spices.

GIN Liquor distilled from rye and other grains and flavored with juniper berries.

GRAND MARNIER French orange-flavored, cognac-based liqueur.

IRISH MIST Irish whiskey-based liqueur with the added flavor of oranges and honey.

IRISH WHISKEY Of the whiskeys, the only one distilled three times.

KAHLUA Mexican coffee-flavored liqueur.

KIRSCHWASSER Also called **KIRSCH**; a black cherry-flavored liqueur.

KÜMMEL Colorless liqueur flavored with caraway seeds.

LILLET Red or white French aperitif wine.

MALIBU RUM Coconut-flavored rum.

MARASCHINO LIQUEUR Almond- and cherry-flavored liqueur.

METAXA Greek brandy.

OUZO Licorice-flavored Greek aperitif.

PEANUT LOLITA Peanut-flavored liqueur.

PEPPERMINT SCHNAPPS Mint-flavored liqueur.

PERNOD Another licorice-flavored liqueur.

RUM Liquor distilled from fermented sugar cane or molasses.

RYE WHISKEY Made mainly from rye.

SABRA Israeli orange-chocolate liqueur.

SAMBUCA Italian licorice-flavored liqueur.

SCOTCH WHISKEY Made from grain and malt; blended and single malt.

SLOE GIN Made from sloe berries soaked in gin.

SOUTHERN COMFORT Liqueur made by combining peaches, peach liqueur, and bourbon.

STRAIGHT WHISKEY Made with one type of barley malt.

STREGA Another sweet Italian liqueur.

TEQUILA Mexican liquor distilled from the sap (fermented) of the mescal plant.

TIA MARIA Jamaican coffee-flavored liqueur.

TRIPLE SEC Another orange-flavored liqueur.

TUACA Italian citrus-flavored, brandy-based liqueur.

VANDERMINT Dutch mint-chocolate-flavored liqueur.

VERMOUTH Either dry or sweet, this aperitif wine is flavored with various herbs.

VODKA Colorless liquor distilled from rye, wheat, or other grain.

WHISKEY From the Gaelic, "water of life." Alcoholic liquor distilled from grain.

WILD TURKEY Bourbon-based liqueur.

WINE Fermented grape juice.

YUKON JACK Canadian whiskey-based liqueur.

HELPFUL HINTS

Before you start pouring, here are a few helpful hints to enhance your mixology skills.

1. Unless you're pouring the ingredients directly into the glass they'll be served in, use a mixing glass and keep your strainer nearby. Not only does this look better but it usually tastes better, as the various ingredients will have been combined more thoroughly. Interestingly, some drinks—the way I learned them—were supposed to be stirred, <u>not</u> shaken. As time went on, I found that most customers *preferred* them to be shaken, <u>not</u> stirred. (Perhaps 007 has been rubbing off.)

2. Unless it is otherwise specified, *always, always, always* chill a cocktail glass before serving a drink in it. This can be done by: a) filling it with ice cubes while you mix the drink, b) filling it with ice water while you mix the drink, or c) refrigerating it for 30–60 minutes before using it.

3. To frost a glass with salt or sugar, use a lemon or lime wedge to moisten the rim of the glass; then dip the rim into a saucer filled with the salt or sugar. Be careful not to press too hard, especially with glasses that have a thin edge. To frost with ice, dip the rim of the glass in water, then place in a freezer for 30-45 minutes. For frosting beer mugs, dip the entire mug in water.

WRONG VERB

At one of my mixology gigs, this one a trendy private party for a Hollywood luminary, I witnessed a memorable event (as many bartenders often do).

The Joker himself, Jack Nicholson, was standing near the bar, talking with a friend when an attractive, very chesty, leggy red-head strutted up to him.

"Do you wanna dance?" she asked him.

After about a 15 or 20 second head-to-toe scan of the ultra-sexy woman, Nicholson flashed a sheepish smile and casually replied, as only Jack can, "Wrong verb."

4. To put ice in a glass, *never* dip the glass into the ice bucket. This is a good way to incur a lawsuit. Always bring the ice to the glass by means of a scooper, preferably made of metal or hard plastic.

Other than those four mixology rules, take your time, experiment, and have fun. Don't toss bottles up in the air or back and forth—this is not the set of *Cocktail* (besides, if you knew how many takes it took and how many bottles they broke, you'd never even consider it.). And don't play around when it comes to slicing fruits and garnishes, blending and flaming drinks, or even cleaning up. I've seen numerous accidents—too many to count—most of which could easily have been avoided, and an overwhelming majority of which resulted in a trip to the emergency room.

Beyond that, use good judgment and keep an eye on those that you serve. Have enough sense, and courage, to know when to say "Enough!"

THE USUAL SUSPECTS

Let's face it, the old standbys will never completely die. There will always be those who prefer the tried and true drinks. For them, no multiple mixes, no bubbling concoctions, no funky-colored monstrosities; only simple mixtures with satisfying tastes—tastes they've known forever and have come to love. So, if you're a drinker who prefers the "old school" of cocktails, this section's for you. Some of the drinks may be slightly modified, as compared to how you may have previously poured them. That is simply because the science of mixology is *not* an exact science. Recipes change drastically from one bartender to the next. If your formulas differ, by all means use them. Otherwise, try them my way.

NOTE: The type of glass recommended for each drink is indicated in *italic* in recipe instructions. (See "Glasses," pp. 15-17.)

ALEXANDER

1 oz. white crème de cacao
1 oz. gin
1 oz. heavy cream

Cocktail; shake with ice, strain. Dust with nutmeg.

ALLEGHENY

1 oz. bourbon
1 oz. dry vermouth
1 1/2 tsp. blackberry brandy
1 1/2 tsp. lemon juice

Cocktail; shake with ice, strain. Lemon twist garnish.

ALMOND COCKTAIL

2 oz. gin
1 oz. dry vermouth
1/2 oz. amaretto

Old Fashioned; pour over ice, stir.

AMERICANO

1 oz. Campari
1 oz. sweet vermouth
3 oz. club soda

Highball; pour over ice, stir. Add club soda, stir.

B & B

1/2 oz. Benedictine
1/2 oz. brandy

Pony; pour Benedictine,
float brandy.

BACARDI

1 1/2 oz. Bacardi rum
1/2 oz. lime juice
3 dashes grenadine

Cocktail; shake with ice,
strain.

BAY BREEZE

1 1/2 oz. vodka
1 oz. cranberry juice
4 oz. pineapple juice

Highball; pour over ice, stir.

For MALIBU BAY BREEZE,
use Malibu rum.

BELLINI

Peach puree or peach
  nectar
Brut champagne

Champagne Glass; pour
peach nectar, add
champagne.

BENT NAIL

1 1/2 oz. Canadian
  whiskey
1/2 oz. Drambuie

Cocktail; shake with ice,
strain over ice.

BLACK RUSSIAN

2 oz. vodka
1 oz. Kahlua

Old Fashioned; pour over
ice, stir.

BLOODY MARY

*For a VIRGIN MARY, hold
the vodka.*

1 1/2 oz. vodka
3 oz. tomato juice
1/2 oz. lemon juice
2 to 3 drops Tabasco
  sauce
2 to 3 drops
  Worcestershire sauce
1 dash each salt and
  pepper

Collins; shake with ice,
pour. Garnish with
lemon/lime slice and/or
celery stalk.

BOCCI BALL

1 1/2 oz. amaretto
6 oz. orange juice
Club soda

Highball; pour over ice,
stir. Splash club soda.

BOILERMAKER

1 1/2 oz. whiskey
1 mug of beer

Beer Mug; down the shot,
chase it with the beer.

BOMBAY

1 oz. brandy
1 oz. dry vermouth
1/2 oz. sweet vermouth
1 tsp. curaçao

Collins; shake with ice,
strain over ice.

BRANDY ALEXANDER

1/2 oz. white crème de
  cacao
1/2 oz. brandy
1/2 oz. heavy cream
Nutmeg

Cocktail (or Snifter); shake
with ice, strain over ice.
Dust with nutmeg.

BRASS MONKEY

*The Beastie Boys made
this one famous!*

3/4 oz. vodka
1/2 oz. light rum
Orange juice

Highball; pour over ice, fill
with orange juice, stir.

BROWN

*also called BROWN
COCKTAIL*

1 1/4 oz. bourbon
1 oz. dry vermouth
2 to 3 dashes orange
  bitters

Cocktail; shake with ice,
strain over ice.

CAMPARI & SOD

2 oz. Campari
2 oz. club soda

Highball; pour over ice,
stir. Orange peel garnish.

CAPE CODDER

1 1/2 oz. vodka
6 oz. cranberry juice

Highball; pour over ice,
stir. Lime slice garnish.

CARUSO

1/2 oz. gin
1/2 oz. dry vermouth
1/2 oz. white crème de
  menthe

Cocktail; shake with ice,
strain.

CHERRY COLA

*also called CHERRY COLA
LOWBALL*

2 oz. rum
1/2 oz. cherry brandy
Cola

Old Fashioned; pour over
ice, fill with cola, stir.
Cherry garnish.

CHI-CHI

*How do you think he
made all those putts?*

1 oz. light rum
1/2 oz. blackberry
  brandy
Pineapple juice

Highball; pour over ice, fill
with pineapple juice, stir.

CLASSIC

1 1/2 oz. brandy
1 tbsp. Cointreau
1 tbsp. maraschino
  liqueur
1 tsp. lemon juice

Cocktail; shake with ice,
strain.

CONCORDE
COCKTAIL

2 oz. cognac
2 oz. pineapple juice
Champagne

Champagne Glass; mix
pineapple juice, cognac,
and ice. Stir and strain.
Fill with champagne.

CONTINENTAL

No Lincoln needed

3 oz. rye
1/2 oz. rum
1 1/2 oz. cream
1 tbsp. lemon juice

Collins; shake with ice,
strain over ice.

CUBA LIBRE

*The "ritzy" name for a
Rum & Coke*

1 to 1 1/2 oz. rum
Cola

Highball; pour over ice, fill
with cola, stir. Lime wedge
garnish.

DAIQUIRI

2 oz. light rum
1 oz. lime juice
1 tsp. sugar

Cocktail; shake with ice,
strain. Lime slice garnish.

DIAMOND HEAD

1 1/2 oz. gin
1/2 oz. curaçao
2 oz. pineapple juice
1 tsp. sweet vermouth
1/2 tsp. lemon juice

Cocktail; shake with ice,
strain. Add lemon juice.

DIANA

3 oz. white crème de
  menthe
1 oz. brandy

Old Fashioned; pour over
ice, stir.

DIPLOMAT

2 oz. dry vermouth
1 oz. sweet vermouth
1/2 tsp. maraschino
  liqueur

Cocktail; shake with ice,
strain. Orange peel garnish.

DORADO

2 oz. tequila
1 oz. lemon juice
1 tbsp. honey

Highball; shake with ice,
strain over ice.

DOUGLAS ON THE ROCKS

2 to 2 1/2 oz. gin
1 oz. dry vermouth

Old Fashioned; pour over
ice, stir. Lemon twist
garnish.

DREAM

Kasim the dream....

2 oz. brandy
3/4 oz. curaçao
1 tsp. Pernod

Cocktail; shake with ice,
strain.

DUBONNET COCKTAIL

1 oz. gin
1 oz. Dubonnet

Cocktail; shake with ice,
strain.

DUCHESS

3/4 oz. Pernod
3/4 oz. dry vermouth
3/4 oz. sweet vermouth

Old Fashioned; shake with
ice, strain over ice. Cherry
garnish.

EARTHQUAKE

1 1/2 oz. rye
1 1/2 oz. gin
1 1/2 oz. Pernod

Cocktail; shake with ice,
strain.

EAST INDIAN SUNRISE

1 oz. brandy
1 tbsp. rum
1 tsp. triple sec
1 tsp. pineapple juice
1 dash orange bitters

Cocktail; shake with ice, strain. Lemon twist garnish.

EGGHEAD

1 1/2 oz. vodka
4 oz. orange juice
1 tsp. honey
1 egg

Old Fashioned; blend with ice, strain over ice.

WHO WAS THAT?

I was tending bar at a funky, hole-in-the-wall nightspot in West Los Angeles one evening when a handsome gentleman, late 30s, dressed to the nines in what appeared to be a custom-tailored three-piece suit, struck up a conversation with me and one of the other bartenders.

His accent and his passion for 007-like Martinis identified him as a Britisher, and during the conversation, he revealed that he was from London and in town on business.

About five minutes into the conversation, an attractive young woman walked up to the bar, sat on the stool next to him, and ordered a drink. I recognized her immediately. Without naming names, I'll just say she was one of the young starlets that used to work on Beverly Hills 90210. (For the record, and in case you still don't know who I'm talking about, I think she was married, and divorced, a few times.) Anyway, the two struck up a conversation and, as bartenders usually do, I overheard a good portion of their dialogue.

She desperately wanted to take him home with her, but he was happily married. She wanted to do wild, crazy things to him in her limo, but he just wasn't interested. According to her, she could have anyone in the bar, but according to him, he wasn't on her list. She said she'd only ask him one more time. He just laughed and ordered another drink.

Well, the young actress stormed off, leaving her half-full glass and the man of her dreams at the bar. I refilled the Britisher's Martini and was about to help another thirsty customer when he said, "The nerve of American women. They just don't take 'no' for an answer."

Before I could reply, he mused, "She did look familiar, though. I wonder who she was?"

EL DIABLO

1 1/2 oz. tequila
1/2 oz. crème de cassis
1 tbsp. lime juice
Ginger ale

Collins; pour over ice, fill with ginger ale, stir.

EL SALVADOR

1 1/2 oz. light rum
1 oz. Frangelico
1/2 oz. lime juice
1 tsp. grenadine
1 tsp. lemon juice

Old Fashioned; shake with ice, strain over ice.

EMPIRE

1 1/2 oz. gin
1/2 oz. apple brandy
1/2 oz. apricot brandy

Cocktail; mix with ice, stir, strain.

FALLEN ANGEL

2 1/2 oz. gin
2 oz. lemon juice
2 dashes crème de menthe
Dash Angostura bitters

Old Fashioned; shake with ice, strain over ice.

FAN

2 oz. scotch
1 oz. Cointreau
1 oz. grapefruit juice

Old Fashioned; shake with ice, strain over ice. Cherry garnish.

FANTASIA

also called FANTASIO

1 1/2 oz. brandy
1 oz. dry vermouth
1 tsp. white crème de cacao
1 tsp. maraschino liqueur

Old Fashioned; shake with ice, strain over ice.

FARE-THEE-WELL

1 1/2 oz. gin
1 1/2 oz. dry vermouth
1 tbsp. curaçao
1 tsp. sweet vermouth

Cocktail; shake with ice, strain.

FAVORITE

3/4 oz. gin
3/4 oz. dry vermouth
3/4 oz. apricot brandy
2 to 3 drops lemon juice

Old Fashioned; shake with ice, strain over ice.

FERRARISTE

also called FERRARI

2 oz. dry vermouth
1 oz. amaretto
1/2 tsp. maraschino liqueur

Old Fashioned; pour over ice, stir. Lemon twist garnish.

FESTIVAL

1 oz. dark crème de cacao
3/4 oz. heavy cream
1 tbsp. apricot brandy
1 tsp. grenadine

Old Fashioned; shake with ice, strain over ice.

FIFTY-FIFTY

1 1/2 oz. gin
1 1/2 oz. dry vermouth

Cocktail; pour over ice, stir. Olive garnish.

FINO

1 1/2 oz. fino (dry) sherry
1 1/2 oz. sweet vermouth

Old Fashioned; shake with ice, strain over ice. Lemon slice garnish.

FLAMINGO

2 oz. gin
3/4 oz. apricot brandy
1 tbsp. lime juice
1 tsp. grenadine

Cocktail; shake with ice,
strain.

FLORIDA

3 oz. orange juice
3/4 oz. gin
1 tsp. kirschwasser
1 tsp. triple sec
1 tsp. lemon juice

Collins; pour and shake,
strain over ice. Orange
slice and cherry garnish.

FLORIDA PUNCH

1 1/2 oz. dark rum
1/2 oz. brandy
1 oz. grapefruit juice
1 oz. orange juice

Highball; shake with ice,
strain over crushed ice.
Orange slice garnish.

FOG HORN

2 1/2 oz. gin
Ginger ale

Highball; pour gin over
ice, fill with ginger ale.
Lemon slice garnish.

FORESTER

*also called FOREST
RANGER FRED*

1 oz. Kentucky bourbon
3/4 oz. cherry liqueur
1 tsp. lemon juice

Old Fashioned; shake with
ice, strain over ice. Cherry
garnish.

FOX TROT

1 1/2 oz. light rum
1/2 oz. lemon juice
2 to 3 dashes curaçao
   (blue curaçao for BLUE
   FOX TROT)

Cocktail; shake with ice,
strain.

FOXY LADY

*Drink one and let Jimi
play.*

1/2 oz. amaretto
1/2 oz. dark crème de
   cacao
2 oz. cream

Cocktail; shake with ice,
strain. (Dust lightly with
nutmeg if desired.)

FRENCH CONNECTION

2 oz. brandy
1 oz. amaretto

Old Fashioned; pour over
ice. Stir.

FROZEN DAIQUIRI

2 oz. light rum
1 1/2 oz. lime juice
1 tsp. sugar

Champagne Saucer; blend ingredients with 4 to 5 ozs. crushed ice. Pour and serve.

(Use other fruits and corresponding liqueurs for FROZEN FRUIT DAIQUIRIS. Example: 1 to 2 bananas and 1 oz. banana liqueur for a FROZEN BANANA DAIQUIRI)

FROZEN MARGARITA

1 1/2 oz. tequila
1/2 oz. triple sec
1 oz. sour mix
1 to 2 dashes Rose's lime juice

Goblet/Margarita Glass; blend ingredients with 4 to 5 ozs. crushed ice. Pour and serve.

(As with a FROZEN FRUIT DAIQUIRI, use fruit and corresponding liqueur for FROZEN FRUIT MARGARITAS)

GAZETTE

1 1/2 oz. brandy
1 oz. sweet vermouth
1 tsp. lemon juice
1 tsp. sugar syrup

Cocktail; shake with ice, strain.

GEISHA

2 oz. bourbon
1 oz. sake
2 tsp. sugar syrup
1 1/2 tsp. lemon juice

Old Fashioned; shake with ice, strain over ice. Cherry garnish.

GENOA

1 1/2 oz. vodka
3/4 oz. Campari
2 oz. orange juice

Old Fashioned; shake with ice, strain over ice.

GIN ALEXANDER

1/2 oz. gin
1/2 oz. dark crème de cacao
1/2 oz. heavy cream
Nutmeg

Cocktail; shake with ice, strain. Dust with nutmeg.

GIN AND TONIC

2 oz. gin
Tonic water

Highball; pour gin over ice, fill with tonic water. Stir. Lime wedge garnish.

GIN FIZZ

1 1/2 oz. gin
1 tbsp. powdered sugar
3 oz. sour mix
1 oz. club soda

Collins; shake with ice, pour, add soda. Garnish with orange slice and cherry.

GIN RICKEY

1 1/2 oz. gin
1 oz. lime juice
Club soda

Highball; pour over ice, fill with soda, stir. Lime wedge garnish.

GIN SOUR

1 1/2 oz. gin
4 oz. sour mix

Sour Glass; shake with ice, strain over ice. Cherry garnish.

GOLDEN CADILLAC

2 oz. Galliano
1 oz. white crème de cacao
1 oz. light cream

Highball; shake with ice, strain over ice.

GOLDEN FIZZ

1 oz. gin
2 oz. sour mix
1 egg yolk
1 oz. club soda

Collins; shake with ice, strain over ice, add soda.

GOLDEN SLIPPER

1 oz. apricot brandy
1 oz. yellow Chartreuse
1 egg yolk

Cocktail; shake with ice, strain.

GRASSHOPPER

1 oz. green crème de menthe
1 oz. white crème de cacao
1 oz. light cream

Cocktail; shake with ice, strain.

HARBOR LIGHT

3/4 oz. Metaxa
3/4 oz. Galliano

Snifter; pour. Do not stir.

HARPER'S FERRY

1 1/2 oz. dry vermouth
1 tbsp. Southern Comfort
1 tbsp. light rum
1 tbsp. curaçao

Cocktail; shake with ice, strain.

HARVARD YARD

1 oz. brandy
1 oz. sweet vermouth
1 tsp. lemon juice
1/2 tsp. sugar syrup
2 to 3 dashes orange or
  Angostura bitters

Cocktail; shake with ice,
strain.

HAWAIIAN COCKTAIL

also called HAWAIIAN

2 oz. gin
1/2 oz. triple sec
1 tbsp. pineapple juice

Cocktail; shake with ice,
strain.

HUNTRESS COCKTAIL

3/4 oz. bourbon
3/4 oz. cherry liqueur
1 tsp. triple sec
1 oz. light cream

Cocktail; shake with ice,
strain.

HURRICANE

1 oz. light rum
1 oz. gold rum
1/2 oz. passion fruit
  syrup
1/2 oz. fresh lime juice

Cocktail; shake with ice,
strain.

ICEBALL

1 1/2 oz. gin
1 oz. white crème de
  menthe
3/4 oz. Sambuca
3 tsp. cream
3 oz. crushed ice

Goblet; blend until smooth
and pour.

IDEAL

2 oz. gin
1/2 to 3/4 oz. sweet
  vermouth
1 tbsp. grapefruit juice
3 dashes maraschino
  liqueur

Cocktail; shake with ice,
strain.

IMPERIAL FIZZ

1 oz. bourbon
1/2 oz. lemon juice
1/2 tsp. sugar (or brown
  sugar)
Chilled champagne

Champagne Saucer; shake
with ice, strain. Fill with
chilled champagne.

INCOME TAX

1 oz. gin
1 tsp. dry vermouth
1 tsp. sweet vermouth
1 tbsp. orange juice
2 dashes Angostura
  bitters

Old Fashioned; shake with
ice, strain over ice.

INTERNATIONAL

1 1/2 oz. cognac
2 tsp. anisette
2 tsp. Cointreau
1 tsp. vodka

Cocktail; shake with ice, strain.

IRISH WHISKEY AND SODA

1 1/2 to 2 oz. Irish whiskey
6 oz. club soda

Highball; pour over ice, stir.

ITALIAN STINGER

1 1/2 oz. brandy
3/4 oz. Galliano

Old Fashioned; pour over ice, stir.

IXTAPA

2 oz. Kahlua
1/2 oz. tequila
2 to 3 dashes lemon juice

Cocktail; stir with ice, strain.

JADE

1 1/2 oz. gold rum
1/2 oz. lime juice
1 tbsp. green crème de menthe
1 tsp. sugar syrup
1/2 tsp. curaçao

Old Fashioned; shake with ice, strain over ice. Lime slice garnish.

JAMAICAN

1 oz. Jamaican rum
1 oz. Kahlua
1 oz. lime juice
2 dashes Angostura bitters
7-Up

Collins; shake with ice, strain over ice. Fill with 7-Up. Cherry garnish.

JAPANESE FIZZ

2 oz. whiskey
1 oz. port wine
1/2 oz. lemon juice
1 tsp. sugar syrup
Club soda

Highball; shake with ice, strain over ice, fill with club soda. Orange slice garnish.

JELLY BEAN

1 oz. anisette
1 oz. blackberry brandy

Old Fashioned; pour over ice, stir.

JEWEL

1 oz. gin
1 oz. sweet vermouth
1 tbsp. green Chartreuse
2 dashes orange bitters

Old Fashioned; shake with ice, strain over ice.

JOE COLLINS

1 1/2 oz. scotch
1 oz. club soda
3 oz. sour mix

Collins; shake with ice, strain over ice, add soda. Cherry garnish.

JOLLY ROGER

1 oz. dark rum
1 oz. banana liqueur
2 oz. lemon juice

Old Fashioned; shake with ice, strain over ice. Cherry garnish.

JUPITER COCKTAIL

2 oz. gin
1/2 oz. dry vermouth
1 tsp. crème de violette
1 tsp. orange juice

Cocktail; shake with ice, strain.

KAMIKAZE

1 oz. vodka
1 oz. triple sec
   oz. lime juice

Old Fashioned; shake with ice, strain over ice.

KANGAROO

1 1/2 oz. vodka
1 oz. dry vermouth

Cocktail; shake with ice, strain.

KENTUCKY COOLER

1 1/2 oz. bourbon
1/2 oz. light rum
1/2 oz. orange juice
1/2 oz. lemon juice
1/2 tsp. grenadine

Old Fashioned; shake with ice, strain over ice. Cherry garnish.

KINGSTON

2 oz. Jamaican rum
1 oz. gin
1/2 oz. lemon juice
1 tsp. sugar syrup
2 to 3 dashes pineapple
   juice

Cocktail; shake with ice, strain. Add pineapple juice.

KNOCKOUT

3/4 oz. Southern Comfort
3/4 oz. apricot brandy
3/4 oz. sloe gin
3/4 oz. orange juice

Old Fashioned; pour over
ice, stir.

KYOTO COOLER

1 1/2 oz. gin
1/2 oz. dry vermouth
1/2 oz. apricot brandy
1/2 oz. triple sec
1 tsp. grenadine

Old Fashioned; shake with
ice, strain over ice. Orange
slice and cherry garnish.

LADIES

2 oz. Canadian whiskey
2 dashes Pernod
2 dashes Angostura
  bitters
2 dashes anisette

Cocktail; shake with ice,
strain.

LADYFINGER

1 1/2 oz. gin
3/4 oz. kirschwasser
3/4 oz. cherry brandy

Cocktail; shake with ice,
strain.

LA JOLLA

1 1/2 oz. brandy
3/4 oz. banana liqueur
1 tbsp. lemon juice
1 tsp. orange juice

Cocktail; shake with ice,
strain.

LEAP YEAR

1 1/2 oz. gin
1/2 oz. Grand Marnier
1/2 oz. sweet vermouth
1 tsp. lemon juice

Cocktail; shake with ice,
strain.

LEPRECHAUN

2 1/2 oz. Irish whiskey
Tonic water

Old Fashioned; pour
whiskey over ice, fill with
tonic water, stir. Lemon
twist garnish.

LIMBO

2 oz. light rum
1/2 oz. banana liqueur
1 oz. orange juice

Cocktail; shake with ice,
strain.

LIME RICKEY

1 1/2 oz. gin
1/2 oz. lime juice
Club soda

Highball; pour over ice, fill
with soda, stir. Lime slice
garnish.

LONDON

1 1/2 oz. gin
2 to 3 dashes Pernod
2 to 3 dashes orange
  bitters
1 tsp. sugar

Cocktail; shake with ice,
strain.

MAI TAI

1 oz. light rum
1/2 oz. triple sec
1/2 oz. orgeat syrup
1 1/2 oz. sour mix

Collins; shake with ice,
strain over ice. Cherry and
orange slice garnish.

MANHATTAN

1 1/2 oz. blended
  whiskey
1/2 oz. sweet vermouth

Cocktail; shake with ice,
strain. Cherry garnish.

For a DRY MANHATTAN,
use dry vermouth and gar-
nish with an olive. For a
PERFECT MANHATTAN, use
1/4 oz. of both dry and
sweet vermouth and gar-
nish with a lemon twist.

MARTINI

1 1/2 oz. gin
1/4 to 1/8 oz. dry ver-
  mouth

Martini; stir (or shake for
007!) with ice, strain.
Olive garnish.

MELON BALL

1 oz. vodka
1/2 oz. Midori melon
  liqueur
5 oz. orange juice

Highball; pour over ice,
stir.

MIAMI BEACH

1 1/2 oz. scotch
1 1/2 oz. dry vermouth
1 oz. grapefruit juice

Cocktail; shake with ice,
strain.

MOCKINGBIRD

1 1/2 oz. tequila
1 tbsp. white crème de menthe
1 oz. lime juice

Cocktail; shake with ice, strain.

MONTANA

1 1/2 oz. brandy
2 tsp. dry vermouth
2 tsp. port wine

Old Fashioned; pour over ice, stir.

MULE'S HIND QUARTERS

3/4 oz. gin
1/2 oz. apple brandy
1 tbsp. Benedictine
1 tbsp. apricot brandy
1 tsp. maple syrup (or sugar syrup)

Old Fashioned; shake with ice, strain over ice.

NEGRONI

1 oz. gin
1 oz. Campari
1 oz. sweet vermouth

Cocktail; pour over ice, stir, strain. Lemon twist garnish.

NEVINS

1 1/2 oz. bourbon
1 tbsp. grapefruit juice
1 tsp. lemon juice
1 tsp. apricot brandy
2 dashes Angostura bitters

Highball; shake with ice, strain over ice.

NEWBURY

1 oz. gin
1 oz. sweet vermouth
2 dashes curaçao

Cocktail; pour over ice, stir, strain. Orange twist garnish.

NIGHT CAP

1 oz. brandy
3/4 oz. curaçao
3/4 oz. anisette
1 egg yolk

Cocktail; shake with ice, strain.

OLYMPIC

3/4 oz. brandy
3/4 oz. curaçao
1/2 oz. orange juice

Old Fashioned; shake with ice, strain over ice.

OPERA

1 1/2 oz. gin
1/2 oz. Dubonnet
1/2 oz. cherry liqueur

Cocktail; pour over ice, stir, strain. Orange twist garnish.

ORIENTAL

1 oz. rye
1/2 oz. lime juice
1/4 oz. sweet vermouth
1/4 oz. Cointreau

Cocktail; shake with ice, strain.

PANAMA

1 oz. dark rum
1/2 oz. white crème de cacao
1/2 oz. cream
Nutmeg

Old Fashioned; shake with ice, strain over ice. Dust with nutmeg.

PANCHO VILLA

1 oz. light rum
1 oz. gin
1/2 oz. apricot brandy
1 tsp. cherry brandy
1/2 tsp. pineapple juice

Old Fashioned; shake with ice, strain over ice. Cherry garnish.

PANTHER

1 1/2 oz. tequila
1/2 oz. sour mix

Old Fashioned; shake with ice, strain over ice.

PARISIAN

3/4 oz. gin
3/4 oz. dry vermouth
3/4 oz. crème de cassis

Cocktail; shake with ice, strain.

PEPPERMINT STING

1 1/2 oz. brandy
1 oz. peppermint schnapps

Old Fashioned; shake with ice, strain over ice.

PICON

1 oz. Amer Picon
1 oz. dry vermouth

Cocktail; shake with ice, strain.

PIÑA COLADA

1 1/2 oz. light rum
1 oz. cream of coconut
2 to 3 oz. pineapple
  chunks (fresh or
  canned)
2 to 3 oz. pineapple juice
1 tsp. light cream
3 oz. crushed ice

Goblet; blend until
smooth. Garnish with
cherry and pineapple
wedge.

PINK LADY

1 oz. gin
1 oz. cream
1/2 oz. grenadine

Cocktail; shake with ice,
strain.

PINK PANTHER

3/4 oz. gin
3/4 oz. dry vermouth
1/2 oz. crème de cassis
1/2 oz. orange juice
1 egg white

Cocktail; shake with ice,
strain.

PINK SQUIRREL

1/2 oz. white crème de
  cacao
1/2 oz. crème de noyaux
2 oz. light cream

Cocktail; shake with ice,
strain.

PLAZA

1 oz. gin
1 oz. dry vermouth
1 oz. sweet vermouth
1 tbsp. pineapple juice

Cocktail; shake with ice,
strain.

POKER

1 1/2 oz. gold rum
1 1/2 oz. dry vermouth
1/2 tsp. lime juice

Cocktail; shake with ice,
strain. Add lime juice.

POLO

1 1/2 oz. gin
2 tsp. orange juice
2 tsp. grapefruit juice

Old Fashioned; pour over
ice, stir.

POOP DECK

1 oz. blackberry brandy
1/2 oz. port wine
1/2 oz. brandy

Cocktail; shake with ice,
strain.

PRINCE

1 1/2 oz. blended
   whiskey
2 to 4 dashes orange
   bitters
1/2 tsp. white crème de
   menthe

Old Fashioned; shake with
ice, strain over ice. Add
white crème de menthe.

PROHIBITION

1 oz. gin
1 oz. Lillet
2 dashes orange juice
2 dashes apricot brandy

Cocktail; shake with
ice, strain. Lemon twist
garnish.

QUAKER

1 oz. brandy
1 oz. light rum
1/2 oz. lemon juice
1/2 oz. raspberry syrup

Cocktail; shake with
ice, strain. Lemon twist
garnish.

QUARTER DECK

1 1/2 oz. rum
1 tbsp. dry sherry
1 tsp. lime juice

Old Fashioned; shake with
ice, strain over ice. Lime
slice garnish.

QUARTZ COOLER

1 oz. vodka
1/2 oz. tequila
1/2 oz. lemon juice
1/2 oz. Rose's lime juice
Club soda

Collins; pour over ice, stir.
Fill with soda. Cherry
garnish.

QUEEN ELIZABETH

1 1/2 oz. gin
1/2 oz. Cointreau
1/2 oz. lemon juice
1 tsp. Pernod

Cocktail; pour over ice,
stir, strain.

RACQUET CLUB

1 1/2 oz. gin
3/4 oz. dry vermouth
2 dashes orange bitters

Cocktail; pour over ice,
stir, strain.

RED DEVIL

1/2 oz. sloe gin
1/2 oz. vodka
1/2 oz. Southern Comfort
1/2 oz. triple sec
1/2 oz. banana liqueur
1 tbsp. Rose's lime juice
2 oz. orange juice

Collins; shake with ice,
strain over ice. Cherry
garnish.

RED LION

1 oz. gin
1 oz. Grand Marnier
1/2 oz. orange juice
1/2 oz. lemon juice

Cocktail; shake with ice, strain.

ROB ROY

1 1/2 oz. scotch
1/4 to 1/2 oz. sweet
  vermouth

Old Fashioned; pour over ice, stir. Cherry garnish.

For DRY ROB ROY, use dry vermouth and garnish with an olive. For a PERFECT ROB ROY, use 1/4 oz. of both sweet and dry vermouth and garnish with a lemon twist.

RUM COLLINS

2 oz. light rum
1 tsp. sugar syrup
1 tbsp. lime juice
Club soda

Collins; pour over ice, stir. Fill with club soda. Lime slice garnish.

RUSSIAN

1 oz. gin
1 oz. vodka
1 oz. white crème de
  cacao

Cocktail; shake with ice, strain.

RUSSIAN ROSE

2 oz. vodka
2 tbsp. grenadine
2 dashes orange bitters

Cocktail; shake with ice, strain.

RUSTY NAIL

2 oz. scotch
1 oz. Drambuie

Old Fashioned; pour over ice, stir.

SAKETINI

2 1/2 oz. gin
1/2 oz. sake

Old Fashioned; pour over ice, stir. Lemon twist garnish.

SAN SEBASTIAN

1 oz. gin
1 tbsp. grapefruit juice
1 tbsp. lemon juice
1 tsp. triple sec
1 tsp. light rum

Cocktail; shake with ice, strain.

SCORPION

2 oz. light rum
1 oz. brandy
2 oz. orange juice
1/2 oz. lemon juice
1/2 oz. crème de noyaux
3 oz. crushed ice

Highball; blend until smooth. Orange slice garnish.

SEVEN AND SEVEN

1 1/2 to 2 oz. Seagram's 7 blended whiskey
7-Up

Highball; pour over ice, stir. Cherry garnish.

SEVILLE

1 1/2 oz. gin
1/2 oz. fino (dry) sherry
1/2 oz. lemon juice
1/2 oz. orange juice
1 tsp. sugar syrup

Old Fashioned; shake with ice, strain over ice.

SHANGHAI

1 1/2 oz. dark rum
1 oz. Sambuca
1/2 oz. lemon juice
1 tsp. grenadine

Cocktail; shake with ice, strain.

SKIP AND GO NAKED

1 oz. gin
2 oz. sour mix
Cold beer

Collins; pour gin and sour mix over ice, fill with beer, stir.

SLEEPYHEAD

3 oz. brandy
Ginger ale

Old Fashioned; pour brandy over ice, fill with ginger ale. Orange twist garnish.

SLOE BRANDY

2 oz. brandy
1/2 oz. sloe gin
1 tsp. lemon juice

Cocktail; shake with ice, strain.

SLOE TEQUILA

2 oz. tequila
1/2 oz. sloe gin
1 tsp. lime juice

Cocktail; shake with ice, strain.

SOUTHERN GIN

2 1/2 oz. gin
2 dashes orange bitters
3 drops curaçao

Cocktail; shake with ice,
strain.

SOVIET

*also called SOVIET
COCKTAIL*

1 1/2 oz. vodka
1/2 oz. amontillado
  (medium dry) sherry
1/2 oz. dry vermouth

Cocktail; shake with ice.

SPHINX

2 oz. gin
2 tsp. sweet vermouth
2 tsp. dry vermouth

Cocktail; shake with ice,
strain. Lemon slice
garnish.

STAR

1 1/2 oz. brandy
1 1/2 oz. sweet vermouth
2 to 3 dashes orange
  bitters

Cocktail; shake with ice,
strain.

STONEWALL

2 oz. apple cider
1 oz. Jamaican rum

Old Fashioned; shake with
ice, strain over ice.

SWEET

2 oz. amaretto
1 oz. Kahlua
1/2 oz. Frangelico

Old Fashioned; pour over
ice, stir gently.

TANGO

1 1/2 oz. gin
3/4 oz. orange juice
1/2 oz. dry vermouth
1/4 oz. sweet vermouth
2 to 3 dashes curaçao

Old Fashioned; shake with
ice, strain over ice.

TEMPTATION

2 oz. blended whiskey
1/4 oz. triple sec
1/4 oz. Pernod
1/4 oz. Dubonnet

Cocktail; shake with ice,
strain.

TEMPTER

1 1/2 oz. port wine
1 1/2 oz. apricot brandy

Old Fashioned; shake with
ice, strain over ice.

TENNESSEE

2 1/2 oz. rye
1/2 oz. maraschino
liqueur
1/2 oz. lemon juice

Old Fashioned; shake with
ice, strain over ice.

TEQUILA GIMLET

1 1/2 oz. tequila
1 oz. Rose's lime juice

Old Fashioned; pour over
ice, stir. Lime wedge
garnish.

TEQUILA MARTINI

2 oz. tequila
1/2 oz. dry vermouth

Old Fashioned; pour over
ice, stir. Orange twist
garnish.

TEQUILA SCREWDRIVER

*For classic SCREWDRIVER,
use gin instead of
tequila.*

1 1/2 oz. tequila
Orange juice

Highball; pour tequila over
ice, fill with o.j., stir.

TEQUILA SUNRISE

1 1/2 oz. tequila
1/2 oz. grenadine
2 to 3 dashes lime juice
2 drops lemon juice
Orange juice

Highball; pour tequila,
lime and lemon juice over
ice. Fill with o.j. Add
grenadine.

THUNDER

2 oz. brandy
1 tsp. sugar syrup
1 egg yolk
Dash cayenne pepper

Old Fashioned; shake with
ice, strain over ice.

TIPPERARY

1 oz. Irish whiskey
1 oz. green Chartreuse
1 oz. sweet vermouth

Cocktail; shake with ice,
strain.

TOM COLLINS

1 oz. gin
2 oz. sour mix
Club soda

Collins; pour over ice, fill
with club soda, stir.
Cherry garnish.

TRADE WINDS

2 oz. gold rum
1/2 oz. plum brandy
1/2 oz. lime juice
1 tbsp. sugar syrup
3 oz. crushed ice

Red Wine Glass (or goblet); blend until smooth, pour. Pineapple slice garnish.

TROPICAL COCKTAIL

3/4 oz. white crème de cacao
3/4 oz. maraschino liqueur
3/4 oz. dry vermouth
2 dashes Angostura bitters

Cocktail; shake with ice, strain.

TURKEY SHOOT

3/4 oz. Wild Turkey bourbon
1/4 oz. white crème de menthe

Snifter; Pour Wild Turkey, float crème de menthe.

TWIN SISTER

1 oz. gin
1 oz. vodka
1/2 oz. dry vermouth
1/2 oz. sweet vermouth
1 tbsp. Rose's lime juice

Cocktail; shake with ice, strain.

UNION JACK

1 1/2 oz. gin
1/4 oz. crème d'Yvette

Cocktail; pour over ice, strain.

UNION LEAGUE

2 oz. gin
1 oz. port wine
2 to 3 dashes orange bitters

Old Fashioned; pour over ice, stir. Orange twist garnish.

VANDERBILT

1 1/2 oz. brandy
3/4 oz. cherry brandy
1 tsp. sugar syrup
2 dashes Angostura bitters

Cocktail; pour over ice, stir, strain.

VICTOR

1 oz. gin
1 oz. brandy
1/2 oz. sweet vermouth

Cocktail; pour over ice, stir, strain.

VODKA COLLINS

1 oz. vodka
2 oz. sour mix
Club soda

Collins; pour over ice, fill with club soda, stir. Cherry garnish.

VODKA FIZZ

1 oz vodka
2 oz. pineapple juice
1 tsp. lemon juice
1 tsp. sugar
Club soda

Collins; shake with ice, strain over ice, fill with club soda.

VODKA GRASSHOPPER

1 oz. white crème de cacao
1 oz. green crème de menthe
1/2 oz. vodka

Cocktail; shake with ice, strain.

VODKA MARTINI

1 1/2 oz. vodka
1/4 to 1/8 oz. dry vermouth

Martini; stir (or shake) with ice, strain. Olive garnish.

VODKA STINGER

1 1/2 oz. vodka
1/2 oz. white crème de menthe

Cocktail; shake with ice, strain.

WAGON WHEEL

2 1/2 oz. Southern Comfort
1 1/2 oz. cognac
1 oz. lemon juice
1/2 oz. grenadine

Old Fashioned; shake with ice, strain over ice.

WARSAW

1 1/2 oz. vodka
1/2 oz. blackberry liqueur (or blackberry brandy)
1/2 oz. dry vermouth
1 tbsp. lemon juice

Cocktail; shake with ice, strain.

WEMBLEY

1 1/2 oz. gin
3/4 oz. dry vermouth
2 to 3 dashes apple brandy

Cocktail; shake with ice, strain.

WHISKEY COLLINS

1 oz. whiskey
2 oz. sour mix
Club soda

Collins; pour over ice, stir,
fill with club soda. Cherry
garnish.

WHISKEY RICKEY

1 1/2 oz. blended
   whiskey
1/2 oz. lime juice
1 tsp. sugar syrup
Club soda

Collins; pour over ice, fill
with club soda, stir gently.
Lime slice garnish.

WHISKEY SOUR

1 oz. whiskey
2 oz. sour mix

Sour Glass; shake with ice,
strain. Cherry garnish.

WHITE BULL

1 oz. tequila
3/4 oz. Kahlua
1/2 oz. light cream

Old Fashioned; pour over
ice, add cream. Stir.

WHITE LADY

1/2 oz. vodka
1/2 oz. crème de cacao
2 oz. heavy cream

Cocktail; shake with ice,
strain.

WHITE RUSSIAN

1 1/2 oz. vodka
1 1/2 oz. Kahlua
1/2 oz. light cream

Old Fashioned; pour over
ice, float cream.

WHITE WINE SPRITZER

White wine
Club soda

Collins; pour over ice, stir.
Lemon twist garnish.

WINE COOLER

Burgundy
7-Up

Collins; pour wine over ice,
fill with 7-Up, stir. Cherry
garnish.

WOO WOO

3/4 oz. vodka
3/4 oz. peach schnapps
3 oz. cranberry juice

Highball; pour over ice,
stir.

XANTHIA

3/4 oz. gin
3/4 oz. yellow Chartreuse
3/4 oz. cherry brandy
  (or blackberry brandy)

Old Fashioned; shake with ice, strain over ice.

XERXES

2 1/2 oz. dry sherry
2 dashes orange bitters

Cocktail; shake with ice, strain.

YALE COCKTAIL

1 1/2 oz. gin
1/2 oz. dry vermouth
2 dashes blue curaçao
2 dashes Angostura
  bitters

Cocktail; shake with ice, strain.

YELLOW RATTLER

1 oz. dry vermouth
1 oz. sweet vermouth
1 oz. gin
3 oz. orange juice

Collins; shake with ice, strain over ice.

ZOMBIE

1 oz. light rum
1/2 oz. triple sec
1/2 oz. crème de noyaux
1 1/2 oz. sour mix
1 1/2 oz. orange juice
1 tbsp. 151-proof rum

Collins; shake with ice, strain over ice. Float 151-proof rum. Cherry garnish.

LOW-TOXICITY FUN & PARTY DRINKS

The drinks in this section are, without a doubt, the best tasting of those listed in this book. Of course, everyone has different tastes, but these are the drinks I'd recommend to enjoy at a party or other social event. In addition, downing one or two of these drinks in the course of an evening shouldn't leave you googly-eyed and stumbling, but again, we all have different tolerances, too.

ABOMINABLE SNOWMAN

This ain't no Frosty.

1 oz. gin
1 1/2 oz. white crème de cacao
1/2 oz. light rum

Old Fashioned; shake with ice, strain over ice.

ACAPULCO

1 1/2 oz. dark rum
1/4 oz. triple sec
1/2 oz. lime juice
1 egg white
Pinch of sugar
Mint leaves

Old Fashioned; shake with ice, strain over ice. Add mint leaves.

ACTION JUICE

2 oz. whiskey
1 oz. dark rum
1 oz. sloe gin
Orange, pineapple, and grapefruit juices

Collins; shake with ice, strain over ice.
Lime/lemon garnish.

ADONIS

2 oz. dry sherry
1 oz. sweet vermouth
2 dashes orange bitters

Highball; shake with ice, strain over ice.

A.J.

1 1/2 oz. apple brandy
1 1/2 oz. grapefruit juice
2 drops grenadine

Old Fashioned; shake with ice, strain over ice.

AMBER CLOUD

1 1/2 oz cognac
2 tbsp. Galliano

Old Fashioned; shake with
ice, strain over ice.

AMERICAN BEAUTY

1 1/2 oz. Jack Daniels
1/2 oz. light rum
1/2 oz. sloe gin
Pineapple juice

Collins; pour over ice, fill
with pineapple juice, stir.
Cherry garnish.

AMERICAN DREAM

2 oz. Jack Daniels
1/2 oz. sweet wine
1 tbsp. brown sugar

Old Fashioned; pour over
ice, add brown sugar, stir
vigorously.

ANGEL'S KISS

1 1/2 oz. Kahlua
1/2 oz. heavy cream

Pony; float heavy cream
on top of Kahlua.

ANGEL'S TIP

*Same as above, except
use dark crème de cacao
in place of Kahlua.*

ASSASSIN

*Sly and Antonio like
this one.*

1 oz. tequila
1 oz. whiskey
1 oz. peppermint
   schnapps
2 oz. cola

Highball; pour over ice,
add cola, stir.

ASTRONAUT

1 1/2 oz. rum
1 1/2 oz. vodka
1 tsp. lemon juice
Passion fruit juice
   (or mango, if available)

Collins; shake with ice,
strain over ice. Orange
garnish.

AUCTIONEER

*Have too many and you'll
hear "Going once, going
twice...."*

3/4 oz. gin
3/4 oz. vodka
1/2 oz. light rum
1/2 oz. Grand Marnier

Old Fashioned; shake with
ice, strain over ice.

AUNT JEMIMA

1 1/2 oz. brandy
1 1/2 oz. crème de cacao

Highball; pour slowly.

BALL 'N CHAIN

1 oz. gin
3/4 oz. light rum
1/2 oz. dry vermouth

Highball; shake with ice,
strain over ice.

BASE HIT

1 oz. vodka
1 oz. triple sec
1/2 oz. bourbon
1 tsp. lemon juice
Cola

Collins; pour over ice, fill
with cola, stir. Cherry
garnish.

BEAN COUNTER

1 1/2 oz. coffee-flavored
  brandy
1 1/2 oz. vodka

Old Fashioned; pour over
ice.

BENT TALLY

1 oz. gin
1 oz. sloe gin
1 oz. apricot brandy

Old Fashioned; shake with
ice, strain over ice.

BIRD DOG

2 oz. vodka
1/2 oz. whiskey
Grapefruit juice

Big Old Fashioned, salt the
rim; pour over ice, fill
with grapefruit juice.

BLINKY

1 1/2 oz. rye
2 oz. grapefruit juice
2 tbsp. grenadine

Highball; shake with ice,
strain over ice.

BLOODY SUKI

1 1/2 oz. vodka
1 tsp. lemon juice
2 to 3 drops
  Worcestershire sauce
1 dollop wasabi
  (Japanese horseradish)
V8 or tomato juice

Collins; Japanese version
of a Bloody Mary.

BLOWFISH

*I wonder if Hootie knows
about this drink?*

1 1/2 oz. gin
1/2 oz. anisette
1/2 oz. dry vermouth
2 dashes orange bitters

Old Fashioned; shake with
ice, strain over ice.

BONGO

2 oz. dark rum
1 1/2 oz. Jamaican rum
1 tsp. banana brandy
2 oz. pineapple juice

Old Fashioned; shake with
ice, strain over ice. Add
pineapple slice.

BOP GUN

2 oz. dark rum
1 oz. sloe gin
Cola

Collins; pour over ice, fill
with cola, stir.

BROKEN NOSE

*Keeps all the Beverly Hills
plastic surgeons in
business.*

1 1/2 oz. whiskey
1 oz. tequila
2 tbsp. cherry brandy
Club soda

Collins; pour over ice, fill
with soda. Add cherry,
lime, and lemon.

BUMP 'N RUN

1 1/4 oz. blue curaçao
1 oz. melon liqueur
1 oz. vodka

Old Fashioned; pour over
ice, stir. Add orange peel.

BURNT SURFER

Malibu's "official" cocktail.

1 oz. dark rum
1 oz. light rum
1/2 oz. white crème de
  cacao
1 tbsp. sugar

Highball; pour over ice,
stir. Add sugar.

BUSTED CHERRY

2 oz. vodka
1 oz. gin
1 tsp. cherry brandy
1 tsp. white crème de
  menthe
Crushed cherries

Snifter; shake vodka and
gin with ice, strain. Gently
add other ingredients.

BUZZSAW

2 oz. light rum
1 oz. bourbon
1 tsp. grenadine
Pineapple juice

Collins; pour over ice, fill
with pineapple juice. Add
grenadine.

CACTUS COLADA

2 oz. tequila
2 oz. cream of coconut
  (or colada mix)
4 oz. pineapple juice

Collins; blend with crushed ice. Orange and cherry garnish.

CARIBBEAN HUMMER

1 oz. light and dark rum
1/2 oz. scotch
1/2 oz. pineapple juice
7-Up or Sprite

Collins; pour over ice, fill with 7-Up. Pineapple wedge garnish.

CASTAWAY

2 oz. dark rum
1 oz. banana liqueur
1 oz. cream of coconut

Old Fashioned; shake with ice, strain over ice.

CASTLE DIP

1 1/2 oz. apple brandy
1 1/2 oz. white crème de menthe

Old Fashioned; shake with ice, strain over ice.

CEMETERY FILLER

1 oz. vodka
1 oz. whiskey
1 oz. tequila
1/2 oz. gin
Cranberry juice

Collins; pour over ice, fill with cranberry juice, stir. Add lime wedge.

CHICAGO BOMB

2 oz. vanilla ice cream
1 tsp. white crème de cacao
1 tsp. green crème de menthe

Old Fashioned; blend until smooth.

CHINAMAN

2 oz. vodka
1 tsp. yellow Chartreuse
Iced tea

Collins; pour vodka over ice, fill with iced tea, float Chartreuse. Lemon garnish.

CHINA MIST

Identical to a CHINAMAN, but use gin in place of vodka.

CIA SPECIAL

1 oz. Irish whiskey
1 oz. dark rum
1/2 oz. vodka

Old Fashioned; pour over ice, stir.

CLIMAX

1 oz. vodka
1 oz. light rum
1/2 oz. apricot brandy
Orange juice

Collins; shake with ice. Lemon/lime garnish.

COCONUT TEQUILA

1 1/2 oz. tequila
2 tsp. lemon juice
2 tsp. cream of coconut
Crushed ice

Highball; blend at low speed, strain.

COFFEE GRASSHOPPER

3/4 oz. coffee liqueur
3/4 oz. white crème de menthe
3/4 oz. heavy cream

Cocktail; shake with ice, strain over ice.

COKE & DAGGER

2 oz. dark rum
2 drops orange bitters
Cola

Old Fashioned; mix rum and bitters, stir, fill with cola, stir. Add orange twist.

CORKSCREW

1 1/2 oz. white rum
1/2 oz. peach liqueur
2 tsp. dry vermouth

Old Fashioned; shake with ice, strain. Add lime wedge.

CORKSUCKER

1 tbsp. port wine
Champagne

Champagne Saucer; fill with champagne, float port.

COUNTRY COFFEE

1 oz. bourbon
1 oz. Southern Comfort
1/2 oz. light rum
Coffee

Mug; pour coffee last, stir.

COW BELLY

1 oz. Kahlua
1/2 oz. dark crème de cacao
1/2 oz. chocolate syrup
Milk

Goblet; Kahlua first, then milk, then other ingredients. Stir gently.

COZY WOODSMAN

The secret to Paul Bunyan's smile.

1 oz. brandy
1 oz. dark rum
1 oz. light rum

Old Fashioned; shake with ice, strain over ice.

CRUISE CONTROL

1 oz. vodka
1 oz. dark rum
2 oz. orange juice
2 oz. pineapple juice
1 oz. cranberry juice

Collins; pour over ice, stir. Cherry garnish.

CUPID'S MISTAKE

2 oz. vodka
1 oz. light rum
1/2 oz. bourbon
1 1/2 oz. pineapple juice
2 oz. cranberry juice

Collins; shake with ice, strain over ice. Lemon garnish.

DALMATIAN

2 1/2 oz. Kahlua
1 tsp. vodka
2 tsp. heavy cream

Snifter; stir vodka and Kahlua with ice. Add heavy cream.

DANCING SPANIARD

1 1/2 oz. blackberry brandy
1 oz. Tia Maria
1/2 oz. sweet vermouth

Old Fashioned; shake with ice, strain over ice. Add lemon twist.

DEVIL'S TAIL

1 1/2 oz. gold rum
1 oz. vodka
1 tbsp. lime juice
2 tsp. grenadine
1 tsp. apricot brandy
Crushed ice

Champagne Saucer; blend at high speed. Add lime twist.

DOCTOR DOOLITTLE

1 1/4 oz. whiskey
1/2 tsp. sugar syrup
1 tsp. lemon juice

Old Fashioned; shake with ice, strain over ice. Add lemon wedge.

DOGFIGHT

2 oz. cherry brandy
1/2 oz. lemon-flavored
  vodka
1/2 oz. anisette

Old Fashioned; shake with
ice, strain over ice. Add
lemon twist.

DORADO SASHIMI

2 oz. dark rum
1/2 oz. tequila
1 tbsp. honey

Highball; shake with ice,
strain over ice.

DOUBLE-TIMER

also called TWO-TIMER

2 oz. whiskey
2 oz. light rum
1 tsp. lime juice
Crushed lime pulp

Old Fashioned; shake with
ice, strain over ice. Add
crushed lime.

DREAMER

1 1/2 oz. apricot brandy
2 tbsp. white crème de
  cacao
2 drops anisette

Old Fashioned; shake with
ice, strain over ice.

DROP-OFF

2 oz. tequila
1 oz. amaretto
Orange juice

Collins; pour over ice, fill
with orange juice, stir.
Lemon garnish.

EARTHQUAKE SLAMMER

*Don't mention this
drink anywhere in
Southern Cal'!*

1 1/2 oz. tequila
1 tsp. grenadine
2 dashes orange bitters
Strawberries or strawber-
  ry syrup
Crushed ice

Goblet; blend with ice. Add
lime and/or strawberry.

EASTER BUNNY

1 1/2 oz. dark crème de
  cacao
1/2 oz. vodka
1 tsp. chocolate syrup
1 tsp. cherry brandy

Old Fashioned; shake with
ice, strain over ice. Float
syrup and cherry brandy.

ELKHORN MALTED

1 oz. Kahlua
1 oz. Frangelico
1 oz. vodka
3 oz. coffee or chocolate
  ice cream
Cinnamon
Nutmeg

Goblet; blend at high
speed. Dust with cinnamon and nutmeg.

ESKIMO'S NOSE

2 oz. brandy
1/2 oz. curaçao
1/2 oz. white crème de
  cacao
2 oz. vanilla ice cream

Big Old Fashioned; shake
well.

EYE-OPENER

1 1/2 oz. light rum
1 tsp. curaçao
1 tsp. white crème de
  cacao
1 tsp. chocolate syrup
1 egg yolk

Old Fashioned; shake with
ice, strain over ice.

FAIRY'S BOTTOM

2 oz. gin
1/2 oz. apricot brandy
1 tsp. grenadine
1 egg white

Old Fashioned; shake with
ice, strain over ice.

FANTASY

1 1/2 oz. brandy
1/2 oz. dry vermouth
1/2 oz. white crème de
  cacao
1 tsp. orange bitters

Old Fashioned; shake with
ice, strain over ice.

FANTASY ISLAND

Where's Mr. Rourke?

1 1/2 oz. Jamaican rum
1 oz. dark rum
1/2 oz. light rum
2 oz. cream of coconut
1 oz. pineapple juice
Pinch of nutmeg

Big Old Fashioned; shake
with ice, strain over ice.
Sprinkle nutmeg.

FERNGULLY

1 oz. dark rum
1 oz. light rum
2 tsp. cream of coconut
2 tsp. orange juice
1 tsp. lime juice
1 tsp. almond extract
Crushed ice

Big Old Fashioned; blend,
strain.

FESTIVAL FOR THE DEAD

1 1/2 oz. blended
  whiskey
1 oz. cherry brandy
1/2 oz. sloe gin
1 tsp. Rose's lime juice

Old Fashioned; shake with
ice, strain over ice.

FINELINE

2 1/2 oz. vodka
1/2 oz. lime juice
1 tsp. lemon juice
1 oz. grapefruit juice

Old Fashioned or *Highball;*
shake with ice, strain over
ice.

FIZZBOMB

1 oz. vodka
1 oz. apple brandy
Club soda

Highball; pour over ice,
add soda, stir.

FLORIDA PUMPKIN PATCH

1 1/2 oz. Malibu rum
1 1/2 oz. white crème de
  cacao
1 oz. grapefruit juice
1 oz. orange juice

Highball; shake with ice,
strain over ice.

FLYCATCHER

2 oz. bourbon
1/2 oz. sloe gin
1/2 oz. brandy
1 tbsp. honey

Old Fashioned; shake with
ice, strain over ice.

FORT LAUDERDALE

A "spring break" special.

1 1/2 oz. rum
1/2 oz. sweet vermouth
1 tbsp. orange juice
1 tsp. lime juice

Old Fashioned; shake with
ice, strain over ice. Orange
slice garnish.

FRENCH KISS

Champagne
1 tbsp. crème de cacao
1 tsp. chocolate syrup

Champagne Saucer; fill
with champagne, stir in
crème de cacao. Float
syrup.

FRENCHMAN

2 oz. brandy
2 tbsp. Dubonnet
1 tbsp. raspberry syrup

Cocktail; shake with ice,
strain over ice.

FRENCH TICKLER

No comment.

1 1/2 oz. brandy
1 oz. banana liqueur
1 tbsp. gold rum

Highball; shake with ice, strain over ice.

FROSTBITE

1 oz. tequila
2 oz. heavy cream
2 tsp. white crème de cacao
Crushed ice

Old Fashioned; blend and serve.

FROZEN GHOST

1 oz. vodka
1 oz. light rum
1 oz. gin
1/2 oz. anisette
1/2 tsp. sugar or sugar syrup
2 oz. cream of coconut

Goblet; blend with ice, strain.

FUZZY NAVEL

1 1/2 oz. peach schnapps
6 oz. orange juice

Collins; pour over ice, stir.

FUZZY PIERCED NAVEL

Shades of the '90s!

1 oz. tequila or dark rum
1 1/2 oz. peach schnapps
6 oz. orange juice

Collins; pour over ice, stir.

GARDEN OF EDEN

1 oz. apricot brandy
1 oz. peach schnapps
1/2 oz. vodka
Orange juice

Collins; pour over ice, fill with orange juice, stir. Cherry garnish.

GEISHA GIRL

2 oz. sake
1 oz. light rum (or sloe gin)
1 or 2 tsp. chocolate syrup
1/2 tsp. grenadine

Highball; shake with ice, strain over ice.

GENTLE BULL

1 1/2 oz. tequila
1 oz. Kahlua
1 tbsp. heavy cream

Old Fashioned; shake with ice, strain over ice.

GINGERBREAD MAN

1 1/2 oz. gin
1 oz. Calvados
1 tbsp. peppermint
 schnapps
Ginger ale

Collins; pour over ice, add
ginger ale, stir.

GLACIER

1 oz. brandy
2 tsp. peppermint
 schnapps
1 1/2 tsp. lemon juice
1 1/2 tsp. lime juice

Highball; shake with ice,
strain over ice.

GLASS SLIPPER

2 oz. vodka
1 oz. light rum
1/2 oz. anisette

Old Fashioned; shake with
ice, strain over ice.

GLINT OF HEAVEN

1 1/2 oz. peppermint
 schnapps
1 1/2 oz. Sambuca

Cocktail; pour over ice,
stir.

GOLDEN CASKET

2 oz. gold rum
1 1/2 oz. Galliano
1/2 oz. sloe gin
Orange juice

Collins; pour over ice, fill
with o.j., stir. Cherry
garnish.

GOLDEN DAWN

1 oz. apple brandy
1 oz. apricot brandy
1 oz. gin
1 tsp. orange juice
2 drops grenadine

Old Fashioned; shake with
ice, strain over ice. Add
grenadine.

GOLDFINGER

*The hell with 007's usual
elixir.*

1 1/2 oz. vodka
3/4 oz. Galliano
1 oz. pineapple juice

Cocktail; shake with ice,
strain.

GORILLA KILLA'

2 oz. banana liqueur
1 1/2 oz. light rum
1 1/2 oz. dark rum
1 1/2 oz. vodka
1 tsp. chocolate syrup
Pinch brown sugar
Mashed bananas
Crushed ice

Goblet or *Big Old Fashioned;* blend at high speed, strain. Banana peel garnish.

GRAPE APE

1 oz. gin
1 oz. vodka
1 1/2 oz. grapefruit juice
1/2 oz. banana liqueur
1/2 tsp. grenadine

Old Fashioned; shake with ice, strain over ice.

GUMBALL RALLY COCKTAIL

Going from New York to Long Beach in a hurry?

1 1/2 oz. vodka
1 oz. blue curaçao
1 oz. sloe gin

Old Fashioned; shake with ice, strain over ice.

GUMDROP

2 oz. cherry brandy
1/2 oz. light rum
1/2 oz. anisette or
  Sambuca
1/2 tsp. sugar syrup
3 cherries

Old Fashioned; shake with ice, strain over ice. Add cherries.

GYPSY

2 oz. vodka
2 tsp. Benedictine
1 tsp. lemon juice
1 tsp. orange juice

Old Fashioned; shake with ice, strain over ice. Add orange slice.

HAIL MARY

1 1/2 oz. whiskey
1/2 oz. dry vermouth
Tomato juice
2 drops Worcestershire

Collins; shake with ice, strain over ice. Fill with tomato juice. Lemon garnish.

HAPPY APPLE

2 oz. apple cider
1 1/2 oz. light rum
1/2 apple brandy
1 tbsp. lemon juice

Old Fashioned; shake with ice, strain over ice.

HARLEM

1 1/2 oz. dry gin
1 tbsp. pineapple juice
Pineapple chunks
1/2 tsp. maraschino
  bitters

Old Fashioned; shake with
ice, pour.

HARVARD

1 1/2 oz. brandy
1 tbsp. sweet vermouth
2 tsp. lemon juice
1 tsp. grenadine

Old Fashioned or *Snifter;*
shake with ice, strain over
ice.

HARVEY BALLBANGER

1 1/2 oz. tequila
1 oz. vodka
2 tsp. Galliano
Orange juice

Highball; pour tequila and
vodka over ice, fill with
orange juice. Float
Galliano.

HARVEY WALLBANGER

1 oz. vodka
2 tsp. Galliano
Orange juice

Highball; pour vodka over
ice, fill with orange juice.
Float Galliano.

HAWAIIAN ORGASM

1 1/2 oz. vodka
1 1/2 oz. light rum
1 tbsp. each green and
  yellow Chartreuse
1/2 tsp. blue curaçao
Pineapple juice
Orange juice

Goblet; shake with ice,
strain over ice. Pineapple
wedge and cherry garnish.

HEADLESS HORSEMAN

*If your name is Ichabod,
avoid this one like the
plague.*

2 oz. tequila
1 oz. sweet vermouth
2 oz. cranberry juice
1 tsp. apricot brandy

Old Fashioned; shake with
ice, strain over ice. Add
apricot brandy.

HIGH-FIVE

1 1/2 oz. sweet ver-
  mouth
1/2 oz. dry vermouth
1/2 oz. sloe gin
1 tsp. grenadine

Cocktail; shake with ice,
strain over ice. Add lemon
twist.

HIGHSTEPPER

2 oz. vodka
1 oz. Kahlua
1 oz. dark rum
1/2 tsp. lime juice
Cola

Collins; pour over ice, fill
with cola, stir. Add cherry.

HOCKEY COCKTAIL

2 oz. Canadian whiskey
1 tsp. brandy
2 drops lemon juice

Cocktail; shake with ice,
strain over ice.

HONEYBEE

2 oz. light rum
2 tsp. lemon juice
1 tbsp. honey

Old Fashioned; shake with
ice, strain over ice.

HORNY MONKEY

Those damn zookeepers!

1 1/2 oz. banana liqueur
1 oz. vodka
1/2 oz. light rum
2 oz. cream of coconut
Pineapple juice
1 banana
Cinnamon

Collins; shake with ice,
strain over ice. Fill with
juice. Add whole banana.
Dust with cinnamon.

HOT MAMA

1 1/2 oz. dark rum
1 1/2 oz. light rum
Coffee
1 tbsp. 151-proof rum
1 tsp. brown sugar
Whipped cream, if
  desired

Hot Mug; pour dark and
light rums, fill with hot
coffee. Float 151-proof
rum or drizzle on whipped
cream. Sprinkle brown
sugar.

HUNTINGTON BEACH

1 1/2 to 2 oz. gin
2 tsp. lemon juice
1 tsp. grenadine

Old Fashioned; shake with
ice, strain over ice.

HURRICANE WIND

2 oz. Malibu rum
1 oz. Southern Comfort
1 oz. mango nectar or
  passion fruit juice
1 tbsp. lime juice
1 tsp. grenadine

Old Fashioned; shake with
ice, strain over ice. Cherry
garnish.

HUSKY

2 oz. Bailey's Irish Cream
1/2 oz. white crème de
  cacao
1/2 oz. light rum
1/2 oz. dark rum
1/2 oz. Kahlua
1 oz. light or heavy
  cream
1/2 tsp. chocolate syrup
Crushed ice (ice cream
  optional)

Big Old Fashioned or *Goblet;*
blend at high speed.

HUSTLER

Larry Flynt's favorite!

2 oz. bourbon
1 oz. orange curaçao
1 oz. sweet vermouth
2 tsp. lime juice

Martini; shake with ice,
strain over ice. Add lemon
twist.

ICEBREAKER

2 oz. tequila
2 oz. grapefruit juice
1 tbsp. grenadine
2 tsp. Cointreau
Crushed ice

Big Old Fashioned; blend
and strain.

ICED VANILLA TEA

1 oz. light rum
1 oz. white crème de
  cacao
1 tbsp. vodka
2 tsp. vanilla extract
  (add more to taste)
Iced tea

Collins; pour over ice, fill
with iced tea, stir. Lemon
slice garnish.

INCA

1 oz. gin
3/4 oz. sherry
1/2 oz. dry vermouth
1/2 oz. sweet vermouth
Dash of orange bitters

Cocktail; pour and stir.

ISLAND NECTAR

2 oz. dark rum
1 oz. gold rum
1/2 oz. light rum
1/2 oz. banana liqueur
2 oz. pineapple juice
2 oz. mango juice
1 oz. cream of coconut

Big Old Fashioned; shake
with ice, strain over ice.
Add pineapple wedge.

JADE COOLER

2 oz. melon liqueur
  (Midori)
1 oz. vodka
1 tsp. peppermint
  schnapps
Club soda

Collins; pour over ice, fill
with soda, stir. Add lime
slice.

JAMAICAN VACATION

Ya' mon', feel the jive.

2 oz. Jamaican rum
1/2 oz. gin
1/2 oz. brandy
1/2 oz. pineapple juice
1 tsp. lime juice
1 tsp. sugar syrup
2 drops banana liqueur

Old Fashioned; shake with
ice, strain over ice. Add
banana liqueur.

JAMMIN' JUICE

*Direct from Syosset, Long
Island.*

1 oz. vodka
1 oz. rum
1 oz. gin
1/2 oz. tequila
1/2 oz. sloe gin
Cola or iced tea

Collins; pour over ice, fill
with cola or iced tea. Add
cherry.

JAZZ

1 oz. brandy
1 oz. black cherry brandy
1/4 to 1/2 oz. lemon
  juice

Old Fashioned; shake with
ice, strain over ice.

JERSEY DEVIL

1 1/2 oz. apple brandy
1 oz. cranberry juice
2 tbsp. lime juice
2 tsp. Cointreau
1 tsp. sugar syrup

Old Fashioned; shake with
ice, strain over ice. Apple
slice garnish.

JESTER

1 oz. light rum
1 oz. green crème de
  menthe
1 oz. cherry brandy

Highball; shake with ice,
strain over ice. Add lemon
twist.

JOURNALIST

also called JOURNALIST'S SOURCE

1 1/2 oz. dry gin
1 tsp. dry vermouth
2 drops curaçao
2 drops lemon juice
Dash of Angostura bitters

Old Fashioned; shake with ice, strain over ice. Add lemon twist.

JOY JUICE

1 oz. vodka
1 oz. light rum
1 tsp. white crème de cacao
Pineapple, cranberry, and orange juice

Collins; pour over ice, fill with juices, stir vigorously. Add lemon slice.

JUMPER

2 oz. green crème de menthe
1/2 oz. vodka
1/2 oz. Sambuca
1 tsp. amaretto
1 tsp. heavy cream
Crushed ice

Old Fashioned; blend and strain.

JUMPING FROG

2 oz. green crème de menthe
1 oz. vodka
1 tsp. cherry brandy

Old Fashioned; shake with ice, strain over ice. Float cherry brandy.

JUMPING JACK FLASH

1 1/2 oz. apple brandy
3 oz. apple cider
1/2 oz. dark crème de cacao

Old Fashioned; shake with ice, strain over ice.

KAHLUA TREAT

2 oz. Kahlua
1 oz. vodka
1 oz. Sambuca
1 oz. heavy cream

Old Fashioned; shake with ice, strain over ice. Add cherry.

KELP GREASE

2 oz. melon liqueur
1 oz. vodka
1 oz. gin
1 tsp. green crème de menthe
Grapefruit juice

Collins; pour over ice, fill with grapefruit juice, stir. Float green crème de menthe.

KEY WEST COCKTAIL

1 oz. light rum
1/2 oz. dark rum
1 oz. pineapple juice
1 tsp. lemon juice
1 tsp. cream of coconut

Old Fashioned; shake with ice, strain over ice.

KICKER

1 1/2 oz. rum
3/4 oz. apple brandy
1/4 oz. sweet vermouth

Martini; pour and stir.

KING

1/2 oz. Galliano
1/2 oz. white crème de menthe
1/2 oz. white crème de cacao
1/4 oz. cognac

Old Fashioned; shake with ice, strain over ice.

KIT-KAT

1 oz. white and dark crème de cacao
1/2 oz. light rum
1/2 oz. Bailey's Irish Cream
1 tsp. vanilla extract

Old Fashioned; shake with ice, strain over ice.

KONG COLADA

2 oz. dark rum
2 oz. light rum
2 oz. banana liqueur
1 oz. white crème de cacao
4 oz. cream of coconut
Crushed ice

Goblet; blend and strain. Pineapple wedge garnish. Serves 2.

LADYFINGER CAKE

1 oz. Bailey's Irish Cream
1 oz. Frangelico
2 tsp. amaretto

Old Fashioned; shake with ice, strain over ice.

LAGONDA

1 1/2 oz. vodka
1 oz. Galliano
Pineapple juice
1 tsp. Sambuca

Collins; shake with ice, strain over ice. Float Sambuca.

LA JOLLA MAULER

1 1/2 oz. banana brandy
2 tsp. white crème de menthe
2 tsp. chocolate syrup
1 tsp. Sambuca

Old Fashioned; shake with ice, strain over ice.

LAYER-CAKE

1 tbsp. dark crème de
  cacao
1 tbsp. apricot brandy
1 tbsp. heavy cream

Pony; pour gently to layer.
Top with a cherry.

LOVE

2 oz. sloe gin
1 egg white
1 tsp. lemon juice
1 tsp. raspberry syrup

Old Fashioned; shake with
ice, strain over ice.

LEMON RUM COOLER

2 oz. light rum
2 oz. pineapple juice
2 tsp. lemon juice
1 tsp. 151-proof rum
Lemonade or lemon soda

Collins; shake with ice,
strain over ice. Fill with
lemonade (soda). Add
lemon wedge.

MAIDEN MARY

2 oz. vodka
1 oz. gin
3 oz. tomato juice
1 oz. lemon juice
1/4 tsp. Tabasco sauce

Big Old Fashioned; shake
with ice, strain over ice.
Add lemon slice.

TOP 20 WORST PICK-UP LINES

*As a Los Angeles-based liquor pourer, I have had the
pleasure—and the displeasure—of being around an
endless array of people. I've met all types and, as is
usually the case with bartenders, been privy to all
forms of conversation. (For the record, bartenders
hear everything!)*

*And since bars and saloons are still labeled and
understood to be "pick-up joints"—rightfully so, I
might add—it will come as no surprise to you that I
have been present during many attempted pick-ups.
Now, the key word in that sentence is* attempted. *I
can't tell you how many individuals—men and women*

alike, but usually men—crashed and burned big-time while trying to procure a date for themselves. True, a great many were successful in their efforts, but compared to those that failed, it's a very tiny percentage.

Often, attempted pick-ups are carried out with only one line or a few sentences, otherwise known as "pick-up lines." Here is a list of the Top 20 most commonly used pick-up lines I've heard that almost always failed. These lines appear in no specific order. In my opinion, they are all equally sad—though some do have a certain, what's the word, ah, yes, primitive charm. (Those are the ones that often resulted in a slap or a drink being thrown in the offender's face.) So, without further delay, here they are:

1. "Your father must be an astronaut because he took the stars from the skies and put them in your eyes."

2. "Your father must be a jewel thief because he stole diamonds from the mines and put them in your eyes."

3. "You must be a model." or "You must be an actress." (In Los Angeles? Hah, go figure.)

4. A woman is sitting at a table, currently alone, with other drinks, currently full, in front of the other seats. A guy will walk up and say: "Hi, are you alone?"

5. "What's a nice girl like you doing in a place like this?"

6. "Come here often?"

7. Staring right at her breasts, he says: "Wow! Are those real?"

8. "What's your sign?"

9. A woman already has a full drink and a man walks up and says: "Can I buy you a drink?"

10. *"Your name must be Angel because you could only have come from heaven."*

11. *"Does a mere mortal like me have a prayer of a chance with a goddess like you?"*

12. *"I've got only one week to live and if I could spend just one night with you, I'd die a happy man."*

13. *"Hi, I'm a producer. Would you like to be in a movie?" (This one will work—but only if you're Steven Spielberg!)*

14. *"Can I pinch you? Nothing so perfect can be real."*

15. *"Did anyone ever tell you that you look exactly like (insert famous name here)?"*

16. *"What's it like to be a flower among all these weeds?"*

17. *"I'm not trying to pick you up, I just picked you out."*

18. *"Is it hot in here? I guess it's just you."*

19. *"Brad Pitt (or another famous actor/producer) is a great friend of mine." (One of dozens of variations used by the name-dropper.)*

20. *"How do you like your eggs in the morning?"*

MAÑANA

2 oz. light rum
2 tsp. apricot brandy
1 tsp. lemon juice
1 tsp. grenadine

Cocktail; shake with ice, strain over ice.

MATADOR

1 oz. tequila
2 oz. pineapple juice
1 tbsp. lime juice

Old Fashioned; shake with ice, strain over ice.

MAUI WOWEE

1 oz. vodka
1 oz. light rum
1 oz. dark rum
1/2 oz. spiced rum
2 oz. mango nectar
2 oz. each pineapple and orange juice
1 tbsp. lime juice
1 tbsp. lemon juice
Crushed ice

Goblet; blend and pour. Pineapple slice garnish.

MAX FACTOR

1 1/2 oz. bourbon
1 oz. cherry brandy
1 oz. sweet vermouth
Dash of Angostura bitters

Old Fashioned; shake with ice, strain over ice.

MELON STALKER

2 oz. melon liqueur
1 oz. gin
1 tbsp. banana liqueur
2 drops cherry brandy

Old Fashioned; shake with ice, strain over ice. Add cherry brandy.

METROPOLITAN

1 1/2 oz. brandy
1 1/2 oz. sweet vermouth
1/2 tsp. sugar syrup
2 dashes Angostura bitters

Old Fashioned; shake with ice, strain over ice. Add cherry.

MEXICAN GRASSHOPPER

1 oz. Kahlua
1 oz. white crème de cacao
1 oz. heavy cream

Champagne Saucer; shake with ice, strain.

MEXICAN MARTINI

1 1/2 oz. tequila
1 tbsp. dry vermouth
1 tsp. vanilla extract

Martini; shake with ice, strain over ice or serve straight up.

MIAMI SUNSET

2 oz. bourbon
1 oz. triple sec
1 tsp. grenadine
Orange juice

Collins; pour over ice, fill
with orange juice, stir.
Float grenadine. Add
orange slice.

MICHELLE

2 oz. port wine
1 oz. pink champagne

Cocktail; pour over ice,
stir.

MIKADO

1 1/4 oz. brandy
1/2 oz. amaretto
2 drops curaçao
1 tsp. crème de noyaux
2 dashes Angostura bit-
ters

Old Fashioned; shake with
ice, strain over ice.

MILLIONAIRE

1 1/2 oz. gin
1 tbsp. Pernod
1 egg white
2 drops anisette

Old Fashioned; shake with
ice, strain over ice.

MINT DELIGHT SUPREME

4 oz. white crème de
menthe
2 oz. light rum
2 oz. white crème de
cacao
4 oz. light cream
6 oz. vanilla ice cream

Cocktail; blend until
smooth. Serves 2.

MISH-MASH

1 oz. vodka
1 oz. light rum
1/2 oz. whiskey
Orange juice

Collins; pour over ice, fill
with orange juice, stir.
Add cherry.

MOONLIGHT

1 oz. vodka
1 oz. white crème de
cacao
1/2 oz. peppermint
schnapps

Old Fashioned; shake with
ice, strain over ice.

MORNING GLORY

2 oz. vodka
1 oz. grenadine
1 tbsp. lemon juice

Highball; shake with ice,
strain over ice. Add orange
slice.

MORNING SUN

1 1/2 oz. gin
1/2 oz. cherry brandy
2 tbsp. grapefruit juice
2 tbsp. orange juice

Highball; shake with ice, strain over ice. Add orange twist.

MUD

Too many of these and your name is....

2 oz. Bailey's Irish Cream
1 oz. Kahlua
1 oz. dark rum
1 tbsp. chocolate syrup

Cocktail; shake with ice, strain. Chill.

NEON BLINDER

1 oz. vodka
1/2 oz. whiskey
1/2 oz. amaretto
2 oz. orange juice
2 oz. cranberry juice
2 oz. apricot nectar

Collins; shake with ice, strain over ice. Add cherry and lime twist.

NERD'S DELIGHT

1 oz. tequila
1 oz. scotch
1 oz. grapefruit juice
1 tbsp. grenadine

Old Fashioned; shake with ice, strain over ice. Add cherry.

NEVADA

1 1/2 oz. rum
3/4 oz. grapefruit juice
3/4 oz. lime juice
1 tsp. sugar
Dash bitters

Cocktail; shake with ice, pour. Add lime twist.

NEW WORLD COCKTAIL

1 oz. vodka
1 oz. dry vermouth
1/2 oz. dry gin
2 oz. tomato or V-8 juice
2 drops lemon juice
2 drops Tabasco sauce

Old Fashioned; shake with ice, strain over ice.

NEW YORK

2 oz. rye
1 1/2 tbsp. lime juice
1 tsp. sugar syrup
2 drops grenadine

Old Fashioned; shake with ice, strain over ice. Add orange twist.

NUT

1 1/2 oz. whiskey
1/2 oz. lime juice
1/4 oz. grenadine
1/2 tsp. sugar or sugar
  syrup

Cocktail, sugar-frost glass;
shake with ice, strain over
ice. Add lemon twist.

NUTCRACKER

1 1/2 oz. Frangelico
1/2 oz. amaretto
1/4 oz. white crème de
  cacao (optional)

Old Fashioned; shake with
ice, strain over ice.

OAR-DRAGGER

1 1/4 oz. bourbon
1 1/4 oz. sloe gin
1/2 oz. sweet vermouth
1/2 oz. lemon juice
2 dashes maraschino
  bitters

Old Fashioned; shake with
ice, strain over ice. Add
orange twist.

OLD FLYING TIGER

1 oz. vodka
3/4 oz. white crème de
  menthe
3/4 oz. Galliano

Old Fashioned; pour over
ice, stir.

OLYMPIAN COCKTAIL

2 oz. cherry (or black
  cherry) brandy
1 1/2 oz. white crème de
  cacao
1 egg

Snifter; shake with ice,
strain over ice.

OPALEYE

2 oz. vodka
1 oz. sloe gin
1 tbsp. cherry brandy

Martini; shake with ice,
strain over ice. Add cherry
brandy.

ORANGE BLOSSOM

1 oz. gin
1 tbsp. dry vermouth
1 oz. orange juice

Old Fashioned; shake with
ice, strain over ice.

ORANGE COMFORT

1 oz. Southern Comfort
1/2 oz. anisette
1 tbsp. orange juice
2 tsp. lemon juice

Highball; shake with ice,
strain over ice. Add orange
slice.

ORCA

Even Shamu would like this one.

1 oz. dark rum
1 oz. light rum
1/2 oz. dark crème de cacao
1/2 oz. white crème de cacao
2 oz. each vanilla and chocolate ice cream

Goblet; blend until smooth.

ORIENT EXPRESS

1 1/2 oz. whiskey
1 oz. sweet vermouth
2 tsp. lime juice
1 1/2 tsp. lemon juice
1 1/2 tsp. curaçao
2 dashes orange bitters

Old Fashioned; shake with ice, strain over ice. Add lemon twist.

PACIFIC PACIFIER

1 oz. vodka
1 tbsp. banana liqueur
1 tbsp. light cream

Old Fashioned; shake with ice, strain over ice.

PAGO-PAGO

1 1/2 oz. gold rum
2 tsp. lime juice
2 tsp. pineapple juice
2 drops green Chartreuse
2 drops white crème de cacao

Old Fashioned; shake with ice, strain over ice. Add lemon slice.

PALOMINO

1 1/2 oz. dark rum
1 1/2 oz. white crème de menthe
1 tsp. chocolate syrup
1 tsp. light cream

Old Fashioned; shake with ice, strain over ice.

PANAMANIAN REFUGEE

2 oz. gold rum
1/2 oz. Kahlua
1 tsp. light cream

Old Fashioned; shake with ice, strain over ice.

PAN-AMERICAN COOLER

2 oz. gin
2 oz. orange juice
2 tsp. orange bitters
2 tsp. maraschino bitters
1 tsp. lime juice
Club soda

Collins; pour over ice, fill with soda, stir. Add cherry and lemon slice.

PARACHUTE

Pull the rip cord!

2 oz. sloe gin
1 oz. dry vermouth
1/2 oz. vodka
Cranberry juice

Collins; pour over ice, fill
with cranberry juice, stir.
Add lemon slice.

PARADISE

1 oz. gin
1 oz. apricot brandy
1 1/2 oz. orange juice

Old Fashioned; shake with
ice, strain over ice.

PARIS

see FRENCHMAN

PARK AVENUE

2 oz. gin
1 oz. pineapple juice
2 tsp. sweet vermouth
3 drops curaçao

Cocktail; shake with ice,
strain over ice.

PEAR PRESSURE

2 oz. pear brandy
1 oz. vodka
1 tbsp. pineapple juice

Old Fashioned; shake with
ice, strain over ice.

PEBBLE BEACH

*Have a few after the
round.*

1 oz. light rum
1/2 oz. whiskey
Orange juice
Iced tea

Collins; pour over ice, fill
with o.j. and iced tea, stir.
Add lemon slice and cherry.

PELICAN BAY

2 oz. dark rum
1/2 oz. Malibu rum
1 1/2 oz. cream of
  coconut
1 1/2 oz. pineapple juice

Goblet; blend with ice at
high speed, pour. Add
pineapple slice and cherry.

PINK FLAMINGO

2 oz. gin
1 oz. vodka
2 tbsp. grenadine
1 tbsp. lemon juice

Old Fashioned; shake with
ice, strain over ice.

POLO LOCO

1 1/4 oz. dry gin
1 1/4 oz. tequila
1 tsp. lemon juice

Highball; shake with ice,
strain over ice.

POLYNESIAN COCKTAIL

1 1/2 oz. gin
1 tbsp. cherry brandy
3 tsp. lime juice

Old Fashioned; shake with ice, strain over ice. Add lemon slice.

PONCE DE LEON

He would've found Florida sooner.

2 oz. light rum
2 tbsp. mango nectar
2 tbsp. grapefruit juice
1 tsp. lemon juice

Highball; shake with ice, strain over ice.

PRINCETON COCKTAIL

1 1/2 oz. vodka
1 tbsp. dry vermouth
1 tbsp. dry gin
1 tbsp. grenadine

Cocktail; shake with ice, strain over ice. Add cherry.

QOOL-AID

1 1/2 oz. whiskey
1/2 oz. curaçao
3 oz. cranberry juice
2 oz. lemonade

Collins; shake with ice, strain over ice.

RACEWAR

Can't we all just get along?

1 oz. white crème de menthe
1 oz. Kahlua
1 tbsp. Bailey's Irish Cream
1 tsp. anisette

Old Fashioned; pour over ice. Stir gently.

RASTA SPECIAL

also called RASTAFARIAN

2 oz. Jamaican rum
1/2 oz. gold rum
1 1/2 oz. cream of coconut
1 1/2 oz. pineapple juice
1 tsp. banana liqueur

Old Fashioned; shake with ice, strain over ice.

REALITY CHECK

1 1/2 oz. vodka
3/4 oz. bourbon or whiskey
2 oz. orange juice
1 oz. grapefruit juice

Old Fashioned; shake with ice, strain over ice. Add orange slice.

RED CLOUD

1 1/2 oz. gin
2 tsp. apricot brandy
2 tsp. lemon juice
1 tsp. grenadine
2 dashes Angostura
  bitters

Old Fashioned; shake with
ice, strain over ice.

RED ROBIN

1 oz. sweet vermouth
1 oz. dry vermouth
1 tbsp. grenadine
2 dashes maraschino
  bitters

Highball; shake with ice,
strain over ice. Add cherry.

REFEREE'S REVENGE

3/4 oz. vodka
3/4 oz. rye
3 oz. grapefruit juice
1 tsp. lemon juice

Old Fashioned; shake with
ice, strain over ice.

ROAD RUNNER

A Scottsdale favorite.

1 oz. tequila
1 oz. orange curaçao
1 tbsp. lemon juice
1 tbsp. lime juice
2 drops blackberry
  brandy

Old Fashioned; shake with
ice, strain over ice. Add
blackberry brandy.

ROLE-PLAYER

2 oz. sweet vermouth
1/2 oz. vodka
1 tbsp. curaçao
2 tbsp. cranberry juice
2 tbsp. apple juice

Old Fashioned; shake with
ice, strain over ice. Add
orange peel.

ROMULAC

*Todd Miller's favorite
drink.*

1 oz. rye
1 oz. sweet vermouth
1/2 oz. maraschino
  liqueur

Highball; shake with ice,
strain over ice. Add cherry.

ROOTBEER TWIST

1/2 oz. Kahlua
1/2 oz. rootbeer
1/2 tsp. powdered ginger
Cold beer

Beer Mug; add ingredients, pour beer, stir. Add lemon slice.

ROSEWATER

2 oz. vodka
1 tbsp. grenadine
2 drops lemon juice

Highball; shake with ice, strain over ice.

RUMRUNNER

1 1/2 oz. light rum
1 tbsp. orange juice
2 tsp. lime juice
1 1/2 tsp. sugar syrup
2 dashes orange bitters

Old Fashioned; shake with ice, strain over ice. Add orange twist.

RUMRUNNER DELUXE

1 oz. dark rum
1 oz. light rum
1/2 oz. gold rum
1/2 oz. spiced rum
2 oz. pineapple juice
2 oz. orange juice
1 tbsp. cream of coconut

Collins; shake with ice, strain over ice. Float cream of coconut. Add cherry.

RUSSIAN MISSILE

1 3/4 oz. vodka
1 1/4 oz. white crème de cacao
1 tbsp. 151-proof rum

Cocktail; shake with ice, strain over ice.

SACKER

2 oz. light rum
1/2 oz. Southern Comfort
1 oz. cranberry juice
1 tbsp. brandy
1 tbsp. grenadine

Old Fashioned; shake with ice, strain over ice. Add lemon slice.

SANTA FE

1 1/2 oz. brandy
2 tsp. dry vermouth
2 tsp. grapefruit juice
1/2 tsp. lemon juice

Old Fashioned; shake with ice, strain over ice.

SCAPEGOAT

1 oz. bourbon
3/4 oz. sweet vermouth
2 tbsp. cranberry juice
1 tbsp. orange juice
Club soda

Collins; pour over ice, fill with soda, stir. Add lemon slice.

SLOEPOKE

2 oz. sloe gin
1/2 oz. tequila
1 oz. orange or grape-
   fruit juice

Highball; pour over ice,
stir. Add lemon slice.

SLOPPY JOE

2 tbsp. light rum
1 tbsp. dry vermouth
3 tbsp. lime juice
2 drops curaçao
2 drops grenadine

Highball; shake with ice,
strain over ice.

SNICKERS

1 oz. vodka
1 oz. white crème de
   cacao
1 oz. dark crème de
   cacao
2 tbsp. peanut butter
1 tsp. chocolate syrup
Crushed ice

Old Fashioned; blend until
smooth, strain.

SOGGY DOG

*Bennington would've
liked this.*

1 oz. gin
1 oz. vodka
2 oz. grapefruit juice
1 tbsp. dark rum
Pinch of salt

Old Fashioned; shake with
ice, strain over ice.

SUGAR CUBE

2 oz. gold rum
1 tsp. sugar syrup
1 sugar cube

Cocktail; shake with ice,
strain. Add sugar cube.

SUGAR 'N SPICE

1 oz. curaçao
1 oz. sloe gin
Pinch of sugar
Pinch of cinnamon
2 drops anisette

Old Fashioned; shake with
ice, strain over ice. Add
anisette.

SUGAR SLIPPER

2 oz. Kahlua
1/2 oz. amaretto
1 tsp. sugar syrup

Cocktail; pour over ice, stir.

SUMMER LOVER

2 oz. apricot brandy
1/2 oz. vodka
2 oz. orange juice

Highball; shake with ice,
strain over ice.

SUNSET

1 1/2 oz. tequila
2 tsp. lime juice
2 tsp. grenadine
Crushed ice

Highball; blend, strain.
Add lime slice.

TABITHA

1 1/2 oz. dark rum
1 oz. sloe gin
2 dashes orange bitters

Highball; shake with ice,
strain over ice. Add lemon
twist.

TAHITIAN SPECIAL

2 oz. gold rum
2 tsp. lime juice
2 tsp. lemon juice
2 tsp. pineapple juice
2 dashes maraschino
  bitters
1/2 tsp. pineapple
  shavings

Cocktail; shake with ice,
strain over ice. Add
pineapple shavings.

TAPESTRY

2 oz. white crème de
  menthe
1/2 oz. cherry brandy
1/2 oz. banana brandy

Highball; pour gently to
layer.

TASER

2 oz. light rum
1/2 oz. dark crème de
  cacao
1 tsp. vanilla extract

Old Fashioned; shake with
ice, strain over ice.

TAX COLLECTOR

also called TAX MAN

1 1/2 oz. dry vermouth
1 tbsp. port wine
1 tbsp. sweet vermouth

Cocktail; pour over ice,
stir. Add lemon twist.

TEAM PLAYER

3/4 oz. tequila
3/4 oz. light rum
1/2 oz. spiced rum
2 tbsp. lime-flavored
  vodka
3 oz. orange juice

Collins; pour over ice, stir.
Add lemon slice and cherry.

TEFLON DON

Mr. Gotti used *to like these.*

2 oz. Galliano
1 tbsp. vodka
1 tbsp. Sambuca

Cocktail; pour over ice, strain.

TEMPEST

2 1/4 oz. vodka
1 1/2 oz. orange juice
1 1/2 oz. grapefruit juice
1 1/2 oz. cranberry juice
2 tbsp. rum

Collins; pour over ice, stir. Add two cherries. Float rum.

TEQUILA SHEILA

2 1/2 oz. tequila
1 tbsp. sweet vermouth
1 tbsp. dark rum
1 tsp. honey
1 tsp. lemon juice

Old Fashioned; shake with ice, strain over ice.

THUNDERBIRD

2 oz. bourbon
2 tbsp. banana brandy
1 oz. heavy cream

Old Fashioned; shake with ice, strain over ice.

TIGER'S TAIL

1 1/2 oz. port wine
6 oz. orange juice

Big Old Fashioned; pour over ice, stir. Add lime slice.

TREASURE ISLAND

Young Jim Hawkins' personal *choice.*

1 oz. Jamaican rum
1 oz. spiced or gold rum
1/4 oz. orange curaçao
1/4 oz. peach brandy
2 tbsp. lime juice
1 tsp. sugar syrup
2 oz. pineapple juice
2 drops Angostura bitters

Old Fashioned; shake with ice, strain.

TROPICAL ISLAND

2 oz. Malibu rum
1 oz. pineapple juice
1 oz. mango nectar

Old Fashioned; shake with ice, strain over ice. Add cherry.

TWO-TIMER

see *DOUBLE-TIMER*

UNDER THE WEATHER

2 oz. dark rum
1 1/2 oz. pineapple juice
1 1/2 oz. orange juice
1 oz. grapefruit and
  cranberry juice

Old Fashioned; shake with ice, strain over ice. Add lime slice.

UP 'N DOWN

1 oz. spiced rum
1 oz. dry gin
2 tbsp. sweet vermouth
1 tsp. sloe gin
2 dashes Angostura bitters

Old Fashioned; shake with ice, strain over ice.

VALLEY OF THE DOLLS

2 oz. apricot brandy
1 oz. orange curaçao
1 tbsp. cherry brandy
1 tbsp. lemon juice

Old Fashioned; pour over ice, stir. Add lemon slice.

VELVET

2 oz. Kahlua
1/2 oz. vodka
1/2 oz. light rum
1 tsp. light cream

Old Fashioned; pour and stir. Chill.

VELVET ORCHID

1 oz. dry vermouth
1 oz. white crème de cacao
3 drops raspberry syrup

Martini; shake with ice, strain.

VICTOR'S VICE

1 oz. tequila
1 oz. light rum
1 tsp. chocolate syrup

Old Fashioned; shake with ice, strain over ice.

VICTORY

2 oz. Pernod
2 tbsp. grenadine
Club soda

Highball; pour over ice, fill with soda, stir.

VIKKI

also called VICTORIA

1 oz. dry vermouth
3/4 oz. sweet vermouth
1/2 oz. grenadine
1/4 oz. orange juice
2 tbsp. lemon juice

Old Fashioned; shake with ice, strain over ice.

VIRGIN

1 oz. dry gin
3/4 oz. white crème de
  menthe
1 tbsp. mango nectar

Old Fashioned; shake with
ice, strain over ice. Add
cherry.

VODKA GYPSY

1 1/2 oz. vodka
1 tbsp. Benedictine
2 dashes orange bitters

Old Fashioned; shake with
ice, strain over ice. Add
orange twist.

VOODOO

*Never mess with Black
Magic!*

2 oz. dark rum
1 oz. light rum
1 tbsp. vodka
1 tbsp. whiskey
2 oz. pineapple juice
2 oz. orange juice

Collins; shake with ice,
strain over ice. Add lemon
slice.

WHITE SHARK

2 oz. light rum
1 oz. vodka
1/2 oz. spiced rum
3 oz. pineapple juice
2 drops grenadine

Old Fashioned; shake with
ice, strain over ice. Add
grenadine.

WILD THING

1/2 oz. light rum
1/2 oz. apple brandy
1/2 oz. banana brandy
3 oz. pineapple juice

Old Fashioned; shake with
ice, strain over ice.

WIRE-WALKER

1 oz. Canadian whiskey
1 tbsp. orange curaçao
1 oz. grapefruit juice
2 dashes orange bitters

Highball; shake with ice,
strain over ice.

WOODSTOCK

1 1/2 oz. gin
1 oz. lemon juice
1 tsp. maple syrup
2 dashes orange bitters

Old Fashioned; shake with
ice, strain over ice.

XANADU

Trust me, the drink is better than the film.

2 oz. light rum
1 tbsp. white crème de cacao
1 tbsp. amaretto
1 oz. heavy cream

Cocktail; pour, chill.

YACHTSMAN

2 oz. cognac
1 tbsp. port wine
1 tbsp. apple brandy

Snifter; pour.

YELLOW BIRD

1 1/2 oz. rum
1/2 oz. each Galliano and triple sec
1 oz. lime juice

Cocktail; shake with ice, strain.

YELLOW FINGERS

1 oz. gin
3/4 oz. blackberry brandy
3/4 oz. banana liqueur
1 oz. light cream

Martini; shake with ice, strain.

YELLOW MONKEY

1 oz. rum
1/2 oz. white crème de cacao
1/2 oz. Galliano
1 oz. light cream
1 banana

Old Fashioned; blend with banana, pour. (Banana peel garnish optional.)

ZERO

2 oz. sake
1 tbsp. grenadine
1 tsp. lemon juice

Cocktail; shake with ice, strain.

These drinks are examples of what can happen when the bar is slow and the bartender gets bored. Too much time on his hands can result in drinks like those that follow. In short, these little jammers are the ones to drink if your goal is to pass out. With some of them, just one will do the trick. A word to the wise: do not drive, jog, pole-vault, or operate heavy machinery after consuming one or more of these dandies. And should you decide to mix them—look out!

ACCOUNTANT'S COCKTAIL

Avoid during tax season.

1 oz. sloe gin
1 oz. bourbon
1 tbsp. pineapple juice

Cocktail; shake with ice, strain, add pineapple juice.

ATHEIST'S PRAYER

1 1/2 oz. tequila
1/2 oz. sweet vermouth
1/2 oz. dry vermouth
2 drops grenadine

Cocktail; shake with ice, strain, add grenadine.

ALARM CLOCK

1 oz. dark rum
1 oz. rye
1/2 oz. Drambuie

Cocktail; shake with ice, strain.

ALEHOUSE SPECIAL

1 oz. rye
Light or dark ale

Beer Mug; drop jigger (shot glass) of rye into ale and drink.

AMY'S LOVER

1 oz. cherry brandy
1 oz. light rum
1/2 oz. sweet vermouth

Cocktail; shake with ice, strain.

APOCALYPSE COCKTAIL

Do you love the smell of vodka in the morning?

1 1/2 oz. vodka
1 oz. calvados
1/2 oz. cognac

Cocktail; shake with ice, strain.

ARIZONA SPECIAL

1 1/2 oz. tequila
1/4 oz. Jagermeister

Shot Glass; why would anyone drink this?

A-TEAM COCKTAIL

Hannibal, Face, Mr. T, and the other guy recommend this one.

1 oz. whiskey
1 oz. cherry brandy
1 tsp. lemon juice

Cocktail; shake with ice, strain over ice, add lemon juice.

AXE GRINDER

1 1/2 oz. tequila
1/2 oz. peppermint schnapps
1 tbsp. lemon juice

Cocktail; shake with ice, strain, add lemon juice.

AZTEC WARRIOR

2 oz. tequila
1/2 oz. dark crème de cacao

Cocktail; shake with ice, strain.

B-52

1 oz. vodka
1 oz. Kahlua
1 oz. Bailey's Irish Cream

Cocktail; add each slowly for a layered effect.

BAZOOKA

1 1/2 oz. bourbon
1 oz. dry vermouth
1 tsp. lime juice

Cocktail; shake with ice, strain.

BEER BUSTER

2 oz. vodka
2 drops Tabasco sauce or raw horseradish
Cold beer

Beer Mug; pour vodka, fill with beer, add Tabasco sauce.

BLACKBALLED

Fraternity got you down?

1 1/2 oz. Kahlua
1 1/2 oz. anisette

Cocktail; pour, stir gently.

BLACK BEAUTY

1 1/2 oz. kirsch
1 1/2 oz. whiskey
Pinch of sugar

Cocktail; pour, stir.

BOSS MAN

1 1/2 oz. vodka
1 1/2 oz. dark rum
1/4 to 1/2 oz. grapefruit
  juice

Highball; pour over ice, stir.

BOUNCING BETTY

1 oz. blackberry brandy
1/2 oz. sloe gin
1/2 oz. dry vermouth

Cocktail; shake with ice,
strain.

BRONX TALE

*A favorite of Chaz and
Bobby D.*

1 1/2 oz. gin
1 oz. sloe gin
1 oz. lemon juice
2 tsp. lime juice
1 tbsp. orange juice

Old Fashioned; shake with
ice, strain over ice.

BUCKING BRONCO

2 oz. tequila
1/2 oz. whiskey

Cocktail; shake with ice,
strain.

BUCKSHOT

1 oz. vodka
1 oz. gin
Black pepper

Cocktail; shake with ice,
strain. Top with black
pepper.

BURP 'N SQUIRT

1 1/2 oz. Jagermeister
1 1/2 oz. dark rum

Cocktail; pour, drink, and
back away!

BUSHDIVER

2 oz. Kahlua
1 oz. Bailey's Irish Cream
1/2 oz. apple brandy

Cocktail; chill apple brandy
before adding.

CAKEWALK

1 1/2 oz. Bailey's Irish
  Cream
1 1/2 oz. Frangelico

Cocktail; pour gently to
layer.

CHAMBERED ROUND

1 1/2 oz. vodka
1 1/2 oz. tequila
1 olive

Cocktail; add olive last.

COBRA VENOM

2 oz. tequila
1 tbsp. dry gin
1 tbsp. lemon juice

Cocktail; shake with ice,
strain.

COLORADO BULLDOG

1/2 oz. Bailey's Irish
  Cream
1/2 oz. Kahlua
Cold beer

Beer Mug; fill with beer,
drop in shot glass contain-
ing Bailey's and Kahlua.

COUNTRY GIRL

2 oz. bourbon
1 oz. Southern Comfort
1/2 oz. lemon juice
1 tsp. grenadine

Old Fashioned; shake with
ice, strain over ice. Add
cherry.

CROP DUSTER

1 oz. bourbon
1 oz. dark rum
1/2 oz. Southern Comfort

Cocktail; shake with ice,
strain.

CROSS-EYED STEVE

2 oz. tequila
1 oz. sloe gin
1/2 oz. grapefruit juice

Highball; shake with ice,
strain over ice.

CRUISER'S DELIGHT

1 oz. Jagermeister
Cold beer

Beer Mug; fill with beer.
Drop in Jager shot.

DARE COCKTAIL

3/4 oz. dry vermouth
3/4 oz. dry gin
1 tbsp. apricot brandy
1 tsp. lemon or lime
  juice

Old Fashioned; shake with
ice, strain over ice.

DEPTH CHARGE

1 oz. gin
2 oz. dark rum
1 tsp. 151-proof rum

Cocktail; shake with ice,
strain. Float 151-proof rum.

DEVIL'S HELPER

Even Satan needs a friend.

1 oz. tequila
1 oz. vodka
2 tsp. sweet vermouth
1 tbsp. orange juice
2 or 3 drops Tabasco
  sauce

Highball; shake with ice,
strain over ice.

DICE THROWER

1 oz. scotch
1 oz. rye

Cocktail; shake with ice,
strain.

DUNCE CAP

1 1/2 oz. gin
1 oz. vodka
1 tsp. raspberry syrup

Cocktail; shake with ice,
strain.

DUSTY ROAD

1 oz. tequila
1 oz. light rum
1 oz. crème de cacao
Cola

Collins; pour over ice, fill
with cola, stir.

EINSTEIN'S BRAIN

1 1/2 oz. vodka
1 1/2 oz. gin
1 drop cherry brandy
1 tsp. grenadine

Cocktail; shake with ice,
strain. Add brandy,
grenadine.

EMPIRE OF DECEPTION

1 oz. light rum
1/2 oz. crème de noyaux
1/2 oz. Southern Comfort

Highball; shake with ice,
strain over ice. Add cherry.

ESTROGEN INJECTION

*also called ESTROGEN
COCKTAIL*

1 1/2 oz. tequila
1 1/2 oz. sloe gin

Cocktail; shake with ice,
strain.

EVELYN'S SECRET

1 oz. apricot brandy
1 oz. vodka

Cocktail; shake with ice,
strain. Add cherry.

EVERGLADES SPECIAL

1 oz. light rum
1 oz. white crème de
cacao
2 tsp. coffee liqueur

Cocktail; shake with ice,
strain over ice.

EXORCIST COCKTAIL

*If your head spins around,
don't blame me.*

1 1/2 oz. tequila
3/4 oz. blue curaçao
3/4 oz. lime juice

Cocktail; shake with ice,
strain.

EXPOSITION BOULEVARD

1 1/4 oz. dry vermouth
1 oz. cherry brandy
3/4 oz. sloe gin

Cocktail; shake with ice,
strain.

FALSE HOPE

2 oz. tequila
1 oz. sloe gin
1 tsp. grenadine

Highball; shake with ice,
strain over ice.

FAXER

1 1/2 oz. vodka
1 oz. sweet vermouth

Cocktail; shake with ice,
strain.

FISTS OF STONE

1 1/2 oz. tequila
1 1/2 oz. sweet vermouth

Highball; shake with ice,
strain over ice. Lemon
garnish.

FLAMING MYRON

Hangs out on Sunset Strip.

1 oz. vodka
1 oz. cherry brandy
2 tsp. dry vermouth
1 tbsp. orange juice

Cocktail; shake with ice,
strain over ice.

FLESHEATER

2 oz. gin
1/2 oz. vodka
1/2 oz. dry vermouth
2 to 3 drops Tabasco
  sauce

Cocktail; shake with ice,
strain.

FOAM

1/2 oz. light rum
1/2 oz. dark or gold rum
Cold beer

Beer Mug; pour, add beer
last. Do not stir.

FRENCH GREEN DRAGON

1 1/2 oz. cognac
1 1/2 oz. green
  Chartreuse

Cocktail; shake with ice,
strain over ice.

GAMBLER'S COCKTAIL

1 oz. dry gin
1/2 oz. dry vermouth
1/2 oz. lemon juice

Cocktail; shake with ice,
strain. Add lemon twist.

GODFATHER

Brando's secret elixir.

1 1/2 oz. vodka
1 1/2 oz. Sambuca

Cocktail; shake with ice,
strain over ice.

GREEN ROOM

1 1/2 oz. dry vermouth
1 tbsp. brandy
2 drops curaçao

Cocktail; shake with ice,
strain over ice.

GUNRUNNER

1 oz. scotch
1 oz. Drambuie
1/2 oz. amaretto
1 tbsp. gold rum

Highball; shake with ice,
strain over ice.

HIT AND RUN

Wilshire Blvd.'s namesake.

2 oz. gin
1 to 2 tbsp. port wine
2 drops anisette

Cocktail; shake with ice,
strain over ice.

HONEYDRIPPER

2 oz. lemon-flavored
  vodka
1 tbsp. honey

Cocktail; shake with ice,
strain.

HORSE'S HEAD

Check your bed.

1 oz. vodka
1 oz. whiskey
1/2 oz. anisette

Cocktail; shake with ice,
strain over ice.

HOTSHOT

2 oz. vodka
1 tsp. lemon or lime
  juice
1/2 tsp. Tabasco sauce

Cocktail; shake with ice,
strain. Add Tabasco and
stir gently.

HUNTSMAN

1 1/2 oz. vodka
2 tsp. rum
1 1/2 tsp. lime juice
Pinch of powdered sugar

Old Fashioned; shake with
ice, strain over ice.

IRISH COP

1 oz. green crème de
  menthe
1 oz. Irish whiskey

Cocktail; shake with ice,
strain.

ISLAND RAIN RUNOFF

3 oz. light rum
1 tbsp. lime juice
1 tbsp. lemon juice
Pinch of salt

Cocktail; shake with ice,
strain.

JAIL ALE

1 oz. Jagermeister
1/2 oz. dark rum
Cold beer

Beer Mug; pour, fill with
beer, stir.

JOLT

2 oz. dark rum
2 oz. gold rum
1/2 oz. amaretto
Iced coffee

Collins; pour over ice, fill
with iced coffee, stir.

KASHA

1 1/2 oz. vodka
1 oz. blue curaçao

Cocktail; shake with ice, strain over ice. Add lemon twist.

KENTUCKY

1 tbsp. bourbon
1 1/2 oz. pineapple juice

Old Fashioned; shake with ice, strain over ice.

KILLER'S COCKTAIL

1 1/2 oz. tequila
1 1/2 oz. Jack Daniels

Cocktail; shake with ice, strain.

KING'S BEER

1 tsp. sloe gin
1 tsp. raspberry syrup
1 tsp. lime juice
Cold beer

Beer Mug; add ingredients, fill with beer, stir.

KISS IN THE DARK

3/4 oz. gin
3/4 oz. cherry brandy
1 tbsp. dry vermouth

Cocktail; shake with ice, strain over ice.

KISS 'N TELL

2 oz. vodka
1 oz. sweet vermouth
1/2 oz. dry vermouth

Cocktail; shake with ice, strain over ice. Add lemon twist.

KNOCKOUT PUNCH

Iron Mike's secret.

1 oz. gin
1 oz. dry vermouth
2 tsp. Pernod
1 tsp. white crème de menthe

Cocktail; shake with ice, strain over ice.

LAWMAN

1 1/2 oz. tequila
1/2 oz. rye
2 tbsp. lemon juice

Cocktail; shake with ice, strain.

LIL' DEVIL

1 1/2 oz. vodka
1/2 oz. dry gin
1 tbsp. Tabasco sauce

Cocktail; shake with ice, strain.

LITTLE JOHN'S ALE

1 tbsp. chocolate syrup
1 tsp. raspberry syrup
Pinch of brown sugar
Cold beer

Beer Mug; add ingredients. Fill with cold beer and stir.

LITTLE PRINCESS

1 1/4 oz. gold rum
1 1/4 oz. sweet vermouth

Old Fashioned; shake with ice, strain over ice.

LONE WOLF

McQuade's favorite potion.

2 oz. Yukon Jack
1/2 oz. sloe gin
1/2 oz. lemon juice
2 dashes orange bitters

Old Fashioned; shake with ice, strain over ice.

LUST & GREED

A film producer's favorite!

1 oz. dark rum (or spiced rum)
1 oz. scotch
1 tbsp. grenadine

Cocktail; shake with ice, strain over ice. Add lemon twist.

MACE

1 1/2 oz. tequila
1 1/2 oz. dry gin
1 tbsp. lemon juice

Cocktail; shake with ice, strain.

MEGGET

1 oz. vodka
1/2 oz. bourbon
1 tbsp. lime juice

Cocktail; shake with ice, strain. Add orange twist.

MIAMI VICE

Crocket and Tubbs are back in action!

1 oz. scotch
3/4 oz. dry vermouth
1 tbsp. grapefruit juice

Cocktail; shake with ice, strain over ice.

MIDNIGHT

1 1/2 oz. Jagermeister
1 oz. anisette

Cocktail; shake with ice, strain over ice.

MIDNIGHT COCKTAIL

1 oz. apricot brandy
2 tsp. curaçao
2 tsp. lemon juice

Cocktail; shake with ice, strain over ice.

MINT 'N SPICE

1 1/2 oz. spiced rum
1 1/2 oz. peppermint
  schnapps
1 tsp. lemon juice

Cocktail; shake with ice, strain over ice. Add lemon twist.

MISSILE

2 oz. tequila
1/2 oz. sweet vermouth
1 tbsp. lemon juice

Cocktail; shake with ice, strain.

MONTANA HILLCLIMBER

Timber and Cootney lap this up!

2 oz. cognac
1 tbsp. sweet vermouth
1 tbsp. Drambuie

Cocktail; pour over ice, stir.

MOON DUST

1 oz. rum
3/4 oz. Galliano
1/2 oz. lemon juice
1 tbsp. grenadine

Cocktail; shake with ice, strain. Add cherry.

MORON

Drink too many and you'll know why it's called that.

2 oz. tequila
1 oz. bourbon
1 tsp. sugar syrup

Cocktail; shake with ice, strain over ice. Add cherry.

NADINE

1 oz. dark rum
1 oz. light rum
1 tbsp. grenadine
1 tsp. lemon juice

Cocktail; shake with ice, strain over ice.

NASTY 'N NICE

2 oz. tequila
1/2 oz. sloe gin
1/2 oz. orange juice

Highball; shake with ice, strain over ice.

NEWTON'S APPLE

2 oz. apple brandy
2 tsp. curaçao
2 dashes Angostura
  bitters

Cocktail; shake with ice,
strain over ice.

NIGHTMARE

1 1/2 oz. cognac
1/2 oz. bourbon
Club soda

Old Fashioned; shake with
ice, strain over ice. Add
splash of soda.

OAK TREE ALE

1/2 oz. amaretto
1/2 oz. dark crème de
  cacao
Cold beer

Beer Mug; fill with beer
last and stir.

OH HENRY

*also called O'HENRY'S
LEGACY*

1 oz. whiskey
1 oz. Benedictine
3/4 oz. ginger ale

Cocktail; pour, stir.

PHILLY SPECIAL

1 oz. bourbon
1 oz. heavy cream
1 oz. dark crème de
  cacao

Cocktail; shake with ice,
strain.

PMS SPECIAL

I recommend it personally.

2 oz. 151-proof rum
Grapefruit juice

Martini; shake with ice,
strain over ice.

POKER PLAYER'S SPECIAL

1 1/2 oz. rum
1 1/2 oz. white crème de
  menthe

Highball; shake with ice,
strain over ice.

PURPLE BUNNY

1 oz. cherry brandy
1 oz. light crème de
  cacao
1 oz. cream

Cocktail; shake, pour.

QUASAR

1 1/2 oz. bourbon
3/4 oz. sweet vermouth
2 tbsp. lemon juice

Old Fashioned; shake with
ice, strain over ice. Add
lemon twist.

RACEBAIT

1 1/4 oz. cherry brandy
1/2 oz. sloe gin
1/2 oz. grapefruit juice

Highball; shake with ice,
strain over ice. Add lemon
twist.

REANIMATOR'S ALE

*A favorite of
Dr. Frankenstein.*

1/2 oz. vodka
2 tbsp. light rum
Cold beer

Beer Mug; pour vodka and
rum, fill with beer, stir.

RED RAIDER

1 1/2 oz. gin
1/2 tsp. cinnamon
2 drops Tabasco sauce

Cocktail; shake with ice,
strain.

RENDEZVOUS

1 1/2 oz. tequila
1 1/4 oz. vodka
1 tsp. sugar syrup
1 tsp. lemon juice

Cocktail; shake with ice,
strain over ice.

ROPEBURN

2 oz. tequila
1/2 oz. lemon juice
1/2 tsp. sugar syrup

Cocktail; shake with ice,
strain.

SAINT'S PROTECTION

3/4 oz. vodka
3/4 oz. cognac
1 tbsp. lemon juice

Cocktail; shake with ice,
strain over ice.

SANCTUARY

*Brock Pruett is safe with
this drink.*

1 1/4 oz. vodka
1/2 oz. banana liqueur
1/2 oz. pineapple juice

Cocktail; shake with ice,
strain over ice.

SILK

2 oz. Kahlua
1 tbsp. white crème de cacao

Cocktail; pour over ice, stir, strain.

SKY-DIVER

2 oz. tequila
1/2 oz. whiskey

Cocktail; pour over ice, stir. Add cherry.

SLEDGEHAMMER SUZY

1 tbsp. brandy
1 tbsp. rum
1 tbsp. apple brandy
2 dashes Pernod

Old Fashioned; shake with ice, strain over ice.

SNOWBALL

3/4 oz. Yukon Jack
3/4 oz. Rumpleminze

Shot Glass; do not stir.

SUBMARINE COCKTAIL

Prepare to dive.

1 1/2 oz. dry vermouth
1 1/4 oz. gin
1/4 oz. Dubonnet

Cocktail; pour, stir, strain.

TANTALIZER

1 oz. brandy
1 oz. bourbon
1/2 oz. lemon juice

Cocktail; shake with ice, strain over ice.

TEASER

1 oz. tequila
1 oz. vodka
2 tbsp. apricot brandy
1 tbsp. pineapple juice

Old Fashioned; pour over ice, stir in apricot brandy slowly.

TROJAN HORSE

1 1/4 oz. Irish whiskey
1/2 oz. Galliano

Cocktail; pour over ice, stir.

VAGABOND

1 1/2 oz. bourbon
2 tbsp. triple sec
1 tsp. brown sugar

Highball; shake with ice, strain over ice.

VAMPIRE

I wonder if Anne Rice would enjoy this?

1 oz. dry vermouth
1 oz. gin
1/2 oz. lime juice

Cocktail; shake, pour.

VERMONT COCKTAIL

1/2 oz. apple brandy
1/2 oz. apricot brandy
1/4 oz. gin
1/4 oz. Benedictine
1 tbsp. maple syrup

Cocktail; shake with ice, strain.

VODKA STINGRAY

2 oz. lemon-flavored vodka
1/2 oz. green Chartreuse

Highball; shake with ice, strain over ice. Cherry garnish.

WHISKEY ZIPPER

2 oz. whiskey
1/2 oz. maraschino liqueur
1 tbsp. Drambuie
1 tsp. lemon juice

Old Fashioned; pour over ice, stir gently. Use Irish whiskey for Irish Whiskey Zipper.

THROWING STARS

One of the many benefits of being a bartender—especially in the Hollywood community—is the opportunity it provides to meet a wide variety of people: people of all shapes, sizes, colors, and, most importantly, personalities. But of all the people I have met, "Bruce" was a story unto himself.

Somewhere in his mid-thirties, Bruce was a beast of a fellow who stood about 6'4" and weighed a good 250 pounds—all solid muscle. (As a joke, I would refer to him as "meat with eyes.") He wore his hair in typical muscle-head "buzzcut" fashion, and every time I saw him, he was dressed in the same manner:

faded blue jeans and a tattered, cut-off Champion sweatshirt, usually red, black, or white.

Despite his leg-breaker appearance, Bruce was a nice guy. A "gentle giant." And every now and then, when he turned up at a bar I was tending, we enjoyed some interesting conversations.

You see, Bruce was also an actor—not a famous one, although he does work quite a bit, appearing in many direct-to-video B-films, most of which are aimed at the foreign market, and I believe he does some stunt work as well. Also, he wrestled in the glamorous WWF (World Wrestling Federation) for a stint but had to give it up because of a nagging knee injury—an injury that resulted in his being cut from a professional football team.

Anyway, Bruce was an actor and, as actors often do, we talked about the industry and films and scripts and other Hollywoodesque topics. But Bruce and I also shared another common interest. It seems we both had an affinity for weapons and martial arts.

One night, after ordering one of his "usual" elixirs—an Alice In Wonderland, always with a beer chaser—he told me of a new hobby he had acquired. He said he'd become very interested in Throwing Stars and, without trying to brag, said he was getting quite good at it.

Now, for those of you not in the know, "throwing stars," also known as "shurikens," are a variety of edged throwing weapon, usually shaped like a 3-, 4-, 5-, 6-, 7-, or 8-pointed star that the martial artist uses for sport or for combat. A traditional weapon, stars are often featured in karate action films and are especially popular among the lower-budgeted films in the genre.

As I had never learned the required technique, Bruce volunteered to teach me all I would ever need to know about throwing stars. However, when he told me to meet him in front of a popular cafe on Melrose Avenue just before lunch, I thought it was an odd place to learn the skill. But I figured we'd just wind up eating first. Man, was I wrong.

The next day, I showed up a few minutes early at the agreed-upon location. Bruce was already there, dressed in his usual faded denims and his torn black Champion sweatshirt, wearing a blue bandanna on his head and an overly anxious smile.

"Are you ready to learn?" he asked with a shit-eating grin.

Still slightly confused, I nevertheless replied, "Sure."

"Okay," he said. "this is how it's done. The first thing you have to do is pick your target." And with that, he began scanning the crowded street as if he were a hunter searching for his prey.

I wanted to question him on exactly what he was doing but, given his immense size and the fact that he was rumored to be a big anabolic steroid user—thus probably prone to mood swings we've all heard stories about—I figured it best to just let him do his thing. I had already done my time with braces, I was not considering rhinoplasty, and a broken limb or two was definitely not what I needed. In other words, I said nothing. After a few minutes of recon, his smile widened and his body tensed. What happened next I'll never forget for the rest of my life.

Already beginning to move away from me, creeping at first like a stalking cheetah, he said, "Technique is the most important thing. Accuracy doesn't count for shit."

His speed increased as he headed for a nearby cafe's doorway, probably about fifteen yards away. There, standing out front, having just emerged from the eatery with a few friends, was a man whose face I—along with many other TV watchers the world over—have seen on the tube for a number of years. (I'd say his name, but I'm afraid I'd get called into court and have to give Bruce's real name and accurate testimony of what I saw, thereby sealing my fate!)

Never slowing, Bruce reached the famous television personality before the valet returned with his car and, with barely any effort, tossed the guy through the air, ass over teacups, into a group of leather-clad Melrose Avenue "townies."

CRASH!

It looked like a bowling ball striking the one-pin and the entire group went down in a twisted heap. Bruce stopped, released a bellowing, guttural roar, hit a double-biceps "Incredible Hulk" pose, and yelled back in my direction: "Thus concludeth the lesson!" before bolting down the street and disappearing around the corner.

I could only stand there in shock—albeit laughing to myself—as I marveled about learning the incredibly exciting new sport of Throwing Stars.

For the sake of all the celebrities out there, I hope this activity doesn't achieve the same widespread popularity as cow-tipping. Otherwise, Hollywood's personal injury lawyers will gain an abundance of new clients.

The other possible heading for this section would be "How Could You Let Me Drink That?" These are the cocktails that get consumed *after* the damage has been done. After all, I find it hard to believe that a sober person would order one of these unholy concoctions because they truly *like* the taste. No, I chalk it up to unintentional self-torture. The bars are full of that these days.

ABRAHAM'S MOTHER

Presidential inspiration in a glass.

1 oz. gin
1/2 oz. sweet vermouth
1 1/2 oz. orange juice
2 dashes orange bitters

Highball; shake with ice, strain over ice. Add lemon slice.

ACID RAINFALL

Greenpeace activists take note.

1 oz. apple brandy
1/2 oz. vodka
1 tsp. lemon juice

Cocktail; shake with ice, strain, add lemon juice.

ACNE CLEARER

1 1/2 oz. vodka
1/2 oz. dry gin
1/2 oz. tequila
1 tbsp. raspberry syrup
Pineapple juice

Highball; shake with ice, strain over ice, fill with pineapple juice, stir.

AFTERTASTE

1 1/2 oz. bourbon
1 1/2 oz. tequila
1/4 to 1/2 oz. Galliano
Grapefruit juice

Old Fashioned; shake with ice, strain over ice.

AGGRAVATION

*also called AGGRAVATED
WOUND*

1 1/2 oz. Kahlua
1 oz. scotch
1 tbsp. milk
2 drops Tabasco sauce
2 drops lemon juice

Highball; fill with ice, add
ingredients, stir.

ALABAZAM

2 oz. cognac
1 tsp. sugar syrup
1 tsp. lemon juice
1 tsp. lime juice
1 or 2 dashes orange
  bitters

Big Old Fashioned; shake
with ice, strain over ice.

A-POSITIVE

2 1/2 oz. tequila
Tomato juice
Pinch of salt

Highball; shake with ice,
strain over ice. Add salt.

APPLEJACK
GUNFIGHTER

1 1/2 oz. apple brandy
1 oz. light rum
1 tbsp. lime juice

Old Fashioned; shake with
ice, strain over ice. Add
lemon slice.

ATOM BOMB

2 oz. vodka
1 oz. dry vermouth
1 tbsp. Tabasco sauce

Old Fashioned; pour over
ice, stir. Add 1 olive, 1
cocktail onion.

BACHELOR BAIT

*The choice of all the ladies
at the Peninsula Hotel.*

2 oz. gin
1/2 tsp. grenadine
2 dashes orange bitters
1 egg white

Big Old Fashioned; shake
with ice, strain over ice,
stir in orange bitters.

BACKFIRE

Blame it on the dog!

1 oz. tequila
1 oz. vodka
1/2 oz. sloe gin
Grapefruit juice
2 to 3 drops Tabasco
  sauce

Collins; pour over ice, fill
with grapefruit juice, stir,
add Tabasco sauce. Cherry
garnish.

BAYOU BROTH

1 1/2 oz. brandy
1 oz. bourbon
1 tsp. lemon juice
Orange juice

Big Old Fashioned; shake with ice, strain over ice. Fill with orange juice. Add lime wedge.

BENJAMIN

2 oz. vodka
1 oz. crème de noyaux
1 tsp. lemon juice

Highball; shake with ice, strain over ice.

BLIZZARD

3 oz. bourbon
1 oz. cranberry juice
1 tbsp. lemon juice
1 tbsp. white crème de cacao

Highball; blend with ice until thick.

BOZWORTH

2 oz. tequila
1/2 oz. vodka
1 tsp. brown sugar
1 tsp. lime juice

Old Fashioned; shake with ice, strain over ice. Add lemon twist.

BROWN OUT

also called PILEDRIVER

1 1/2 oz. vodka
1 tsp. brown sugar or chocolate syrup
Prune juice

Collins; shake with ice, strain over ice. Add cherry.

CHUCK

also called CHARLES, CHARLEY, or CHARLIE

1 1/2 oz. brandy
1 1/2 oz. sweet vermouth
2 to 3 dashes Angostura bitters

Old Fashioned; shake with ice, strain over ice.

CLAM SOUP

2 oz. vodka
1 oz. gin
Clamato juice
Cocktail onions

Goblet; pour over ice, fill with Clamato juice. Add onions. Lemon garnish.

COUNTRY BOY

Did you ever see Deliverance?

2 oz. bourbon
1 oz. Southern Comfort
1/2 oz. lemon juice

Old Fashioned; shake with ice, strain over ice.

CRIB DEATH

1 1/2 oz. tequila
1 1/2 oz. light rum
1/2 oz. apple brandy

Old Fashioned; shake with ice, strain over ice.

CROPSY

Terrorizing summer camps everywhere!

1 oz. vodka
1 oz. tequila
1 oz. gin
2 drops grenadine
1 olive, 1 cocktail onion

Cocktail; shake with ice, strain. Add olive, onion, grenadine.

DEAD BABY BOY

2 oz. vodka or gin
1 olive
1 sugar cube
Tonic water

Collins or *Highball;* a simple vodka or gin and tonic. Tie olive to sugar cube with piece of string or use toothpick. When sugar dissolves, the "dead baby boy" will float to the top.

DEAD GIRL SCOUT

I warned her about selling those cookies.

2 oz. vodka
1 1/2 oz. green crème de menthe
1/2 oz. cherry brandy
Crushed cherries

Old Fashioned; shake with ice, strain over ice. Add crushed cherries.

DEPTHS OF HELL

1 1/2 oz. apple brandy
1 oz. cherry brandy
2 drops grenadine
1 tsp. lemon juice

Highball; shake with ice, strain over ice.

DIABLO

1 1/2 oz. port wine
1 oz. vermouth
2 drops lemon juice

Old Fashioned; shake with ice, strain over ice. Add lemon twist.

DIK-DIK

2 oz. apple brandy
2 tbsp. grapefruit juice
1/4 to 1/2 oz. dry gin

Old Fashioned; shake with ice, strain over ice.

DIRTBAG

Lisa's ex-husband's personal favorite.

2 oz. dry vermouth
1 oz. gin
1/2 oz. bourbon
1 tsp. grenadine

Highball; shake with ice, strain over ice.

DOVE KILLER

Keep this one away from the Olympic opening ceremonies!

1 oz. light rum
1/2 oz. anisette
2 oz. white crème de menthe
2 to 3 drops cherry brandy

Old Fashioned; shake with ice, strain over ice. Add cherry brandy.

EBB TIDE

1 1/2 oz. light rum
1 oz. spiced rum
2 oz. pineapple juice
1/2 oz. lime juice

Highball; shake with ice, strain over ice. Add lime slice.

EGG-LAYER

1 oz. whiskey
1 oz. dark rum
1 egg white

Old Fashioned; shake with ice; strain over ice. Add lemon twist.

ELECTRIC TICKLER

1 1/2 oz. gin
1 oz. sweet vermouth
1/2 oz. Drambuie
Orange juice
Club soda

Collins; shake with ice, strain over ice, fill with soda. Lemon garnish.

EL PRESIDENTE

1 1/2 oz. light rum
1/2 oz. curaçao
2 tsp. dry vermouth
2 dashes grenadine

Old Fashioned; shake with ice, strain over ice.

EMPIRE STRIKES BACK

1 1/2 oz. vodka
1 oz. Kahlua
1 oz. cherry brandy
1 tsp. green crème de menthe

Highball; add each slowly for a coagulated layering effect. Float crème de menthe.

ESOPHAGUS CLOGGER

2 oz. Bailey's Irish Cream
1/2 oz. green crème de menthe
1/2 oz. light rum
1 tbsp. amaretto

Old Fashioned; shake with ice, strain over ice.

EXPRESS TRAIN

1 1/2 oz. vodka
1 1/2 oz. gold rum
1/2 oz. bourbon
1 tsp. lemon juice
1 tsp. lime juice

Old Fashioned; shake with ice, strain over ice. Orange garnish.

FAIRY JUICE

1 1/2 oz. light rum
1 oz. sweet vermouth
1 tsp. curaçao

Old Fashioned; shake with ice, strain over ice.

FAKE BLOOD

1 oz. bourbon
1/2 oz. lime juice
Tomato juice
1 tsp. tequila

Collins; pour over ice, fill with tomato juice, stir. Add tequila.

FAST EDDIE

1 oz. dark rum
1 oz. light rum
1/2 oz. lime juice
1/4 oz. lemon juice
Orange and pineapple juice

Collins; shake with ice, strain over ice. Add lime slice.

FEELERS

2 oz. dry gin
1 tsp. sugar syrup

Highball; pour over ice, stir.

FLASHBACK

1 oz. whiskey
1/2 oz. scotch
1/2 oz. rye
2 tbsp. cranberry juice

Old Fashioned; shake with ice, strain over ice. Add lemon twist.

FLYING HIGH
also called HIGH FLY

1 1/2 oz. gin
1 oz. orange juice
1 oz. black cherry brandy
1 tsp. lemon juice
Dash Angostura bitters
1 egg white

Old Fashioned; shake with ice, strain over ice or serve neat.

FRIGID BRIDGET

2 1/2 oz. light rum
1/2 oz. vodka
1/2 oz. apricot brandy
1/2 oz. crème de cacao
Crushed ice

Big Old Fashioned; blend
at high speed, strain.

FUZZBUSTER

1 1/4 oz. dark rum
1 1/4 oz. brandy
1/2 tsp. brown sugar

Old Fashioned; shake with
ice, strain over ice. Add
lime slice.

GAINER'S INTOXICANT

*The unofficial drink of
Gold's Gym's members.*

1/2 oz. Kahlua
1/2 oz. Bailey's Irish
  Cream
1/2 oz. Frangelico
1/2 oz. Sambuca
Low-fat or nonfat milk
Protein powder, if
  available
2 egg whites

Goblet; blend at high
speed, strain.

GARGOYLE

1 1/2 oz. tequila
1 oz. bourbon
1/2 oz. white crème de
  cacao
1 tsp. grenadine

Old Fashioned; shake with
ice, strain over ice.

GLOOM CHASER

1 1/2 oz. Grand Marnier
1/2 oz. curaçao
2 tsp. lemon juice
1 tsp. grenadine
1 tsp. orange juice

Old Fashioned; shake with
ice, strain over ice.

GO-JUICE

2 oz. vodka
1 oz. crème de noyaux
Pineapple juice
Prune juice

Collins; pour over ice, fill
with juices, stir vigorously. Cherry garnish.

GOLDEN DRAGON

1 tbs. yellow Chartreuse
1 tsp. brandy

Cordial; float brandy.

GORGON'S LAST DANCE

1 1/2 oz. tequila
1 1/2 oz. coffee liqueur
1 oz. vodka
1 tbsp. cherry or black-
  berry brandy

Old Fashioned; shake with ice, strain over ice.

GREENBACK

2 oz. gin
2 tsp. lime juice
1 tsp. green crème de
  menthe

Highball; shake with ice, strain over ice.

GREEN DEVIL

1 1/2 oz. gin
1 tsp. green crème de
  menthe
2 tsp. lime juice
Mint sprigs

Old Fashioned; shake with ice, strain over ice. Add igs.

GYPSY DANCER

1 1/2 oz. vodka
1 1/2 oz. light rum
1 tsp. lemon juice
1 tsp. Tia Maria
1 tsp. orange juice

Old Fashioned; shake with ice, strain over ice. Add orange slice.

HARDHAT

1 oz. peppermint
  schnapps
1/2 oz. white crème de
  cacao
1/2 oz. banana liqueur

Cocktail; shake with ice, strain over ice.

HEART ATTACK

1 1/2 oz. dark rum
1 1/2 oz. sloe gin
1 oz. whiskey
1 oz. club soda

Old Fashioned; shake with ice, strain over ice. Add soda and stir. Add lemon twist.

HEART 'N SOUL

1 oz. Southern Comfort
1 oz. sweet vermouth
1/2 oz. grenadine
1 tbsp. cherry brandy

Old Fashioned; shake with ice, strain over ice. Add cherry brandy.

HIGH FLY

see FLYING HIGH

HOMBRE

1 1/2 oz. tequila
1 oz. dark rum
1 tsp. brown sugar
Pinch of cinnamon

Old Fashioned; shake with ice, strain over ice. Dust with cinnamon.

HOWITZER

1 1/2 oz. gin
1 1/2 oz. Canadian whiskey
1 oz. grapefruit juice
1 oz. cranberry juice
1 tsp. lemon juice

Old Fashioned; shake with ice, strain over ice. Add lemon juice, lemon slice.

ICEBERG'S REVENGE

2 oz. vodka
1/2 oz. peppermint schnapps
1/2 oz. light rum
1/2 oz. white crème de cacao

Old Fashioned; shake with ice, strain over ice. Add cherry.

I DON'T CARE

1 oz. bourbon
1 oz. white crème de menthe
1/2 oz. grenadine

Cocktail; shake with ice, strain.

IGNORANCE

...is bliss.

1 1/2 oz. tequila and vodka
1 oz. Galliano
Grapefruit juice

Big Old Fashioned; pour over ice, fill with grapefruit juice, stir. Pour Galliano.

JAPAN'S REVENGE

3 oz. sake
1/2 oz. dry vermouth
1/2 oz. vodka
1 tbsp. lemon juice

Highball; shake with ice, strain over ice.

JAZZ SINGER

1 oz. vodka
1/2 oz. Manischewitz
1 tsp. lemon juice
Splash of soda

Highball; shake with ice, strain over ice. Add splash of soda.

JEWEL OF THE NILE

2 oz. gin
1 oz. dry vermouth
1 tbsp. sweet vermouth
1 tsp. grenadine
2 dashes orange bitters

Old Fashioned; shake with ice, strain over ice. Add lemon twist.

JUGGERNAUT

2 oz. gin
1 oz. sloe gin
1/2 oz. sweet vermouth
Cranberry juice

Old Fashioned; pour over ice, fill with cranberry juice, stir. Add lemon twist.

JUKE 'N JOLT

1 oz. tequila
1 oz. lemon-flavored vodka
1 oz. light rum
1 tsp. lime juice

Old Fashioned; shake with ice, strain over ice. Add cherry.

JUMPING HUMPER

1 1/2 oz. whiskey
1 oz. dry vermouth
1/2 oz. cherry brandy

Old Fashioned; shake with ice, strain over ice. Add 2 cherries.

JUNKYARD DOG

2 oz. vodka
1 oz. tequila
1 oz. dark rum
1 tsp. 151-proof rum
Grapefruit juice

Old Fashioned, salt the rim; shake with ice, strain over ice. Float 151-proof rum.

KAT ATTACK

1 oz. tequila
1 oz. sloe gin
1 oz. sweet vermouth
1 tbsp. dry vermouth or
   1 tbsp. port wine

Old Fashioned; shake with ice, strain over ice. Add dry vermouth or port wine.

KENTUCKY WINDAGE

2 oz. bourbon
1 tsp. lime juice
Lemonade

Collins; pour over ice, fill with lemonade, stir.

KRYOFLUID

2 oz. spiced rum
1 oz. lemon-flavored vodka
1/2 oz. orange curaçao
2 tbsp. grapefruit juice

Old Fashioned; shake with ice, strain over ice.

117

LAKEWATER

1 1/2 oz. tequila
1/2 oz. gin
1/2 oz. lemon juice

Cocktail; shake with ice,
strain over ice.

LAS VEGAS EXPRESS

2 oz. scotch
1/2 oz. sloe gin
1/2 oz. sweet vermouth
1/2 tsp. maraschino
  bitters

Old Fashioned; shake with
ice, strain over ice. Add
lemon twist.

LEMMEHAVEIT

You'll wish you didn't.

1 oz. vodka
1 oz. tequila
1/2 oz. sweet vermouth
1/2 oz. sloe gin
Cola

Old Fashioned; shake with
ice, strain over ice. Splash
with cola.

LEPRECHAUN'S PECKER

Big and green.

1 1/2 oz. Irish whiskey
1/2 oz. melon liqueur
1 tsp. banana liqueur
1 banana

Big Old Fashioned; shake
with ice, strain over ice.
Add banana liqueur and
whole, peeled banana.

LOGGER'S BREAKFAST

*Pancakes and bacon on
the side.*

1 1/2 oz. whiskey
1 1/2 oz. cognac
1 egg

Old Fashioned; shake with
ice, strain over ice.

LONE RANGER

1 oz. tequila
1 oz. gin
1/2 oz. lime juice
Pinch of salt

Highball; shake with ice,
strain over ice. Add lemon
twist.

LOS ANGELES COCKTAIL

1 1/2 oz. whiskey
1/2 oz. sweet vermouth
1 tsp. lemon juice or
  sugar syrup (or both
1 egg

Old Fashioned; shake with ice, strain over ice.

MAINBRACE

3/4 oz. gin
3/4 oz. triple sec
1 tbsp. purple grape
  juice

Old Fashioned; shake with ice, strain over ice.

MAULER

2 oz. brandy
1 oz. light rum
2 tbsp. chocolate syrup

Old Fashioned; shake with ice, strain over ice. Add cherry.

MCDANIELS

2 oz. Jack Daniels
1 oz. Irish whiskey
1 tbsp. lemon juice
2 dashes orange bitters

Old Fashioned; shake with ice, strain over ice.

MILITARY MANEUVERS

2 oz. vodka
2 oz. brandy
2 oz. dark rum
1 oz. banana liqueur
Orange, apricot, and
  prune juice
Crushed ice

Goblet; blend at high speed, pour. (Serves 2)

MILLION DOLLAR BABY

2 oz. gin
1 tbsp. sweet vermouth
2 tsp. pineapple juice
1 egg white
1 tsp. grenadine

Old Fashioned; shake with ice, strain over ice. Add cherry.

MISTLETOE

1 oz. peppermint
  schnapps
1 oz. green crème de
  menthe
1/2 oz. cherry brandy
1 tsp. blackberry brandy
1 tsp. grenadine

Highball; shake with ice, strain over ice. Mint sprig garnish.

MO'

1 1/2 oz. dry gin
1 tbsp. sweet vermouth
1 tbsp. dry vermouth
2 dashes Angostura
  bitters

Old Fashioned; shake with
ice, strain over ice.

MOJO RISING

*I know Jim Morrison
would've liked it.*

1 oz. vodka
1 oz. rye
1/2 oz. scotch
1/2 oz. grapefruit juice
1 tsp. lemon juice

Old Fashioned; shake with
ice, strain over ice.

MOUNT MCKINLEY

1 1/2 oz. whiskey
1 tbsp. sweet vermouth
3 drops Pernod
2 drops cherry brandy

Highball; shake with ice,
strain over ice.

MUDDY RIVER

1 1/2 oz. dark crème de
  cacao
1 oz. Kahlua
1 oz. vodka
3 oz. light cream

Old Fashioned; shake with
ice, strain over ice.

MULE

*Careful, this one has
a kick!*

2 oz. light rum
1 1/2 tsp. lime juice
1 oz. ginger ale

Old Fashioned; shake with
ice, add ginger ale, stir.

NEBBISH

*also called NEBBISH
COCKTAIL*

2 oz. dry gin
1/2 oz. sloe gin
1/2 oz. dry vermouth
1 tbsp. grapefruit juice
1 tsp. grenadine

Old Fashioned; shake with
ice, strain over ice.

NERO

Feel like fiddling around?

2 oz. bourbon
1 tsp. lemon juice
2 dashes orange bitters

Cocktail; shake with ice,
strain over ice. Add orange
peel.

NEW WORLD ORDER

1 3/4 oz. whiskey
2 tsp. lime juice
1 tsp. grenadine

Highball; shake with ice, strain over ice. Add lime twist.

NIGHTMARE SOCIETY COCKTAIL

3/4 oz. gin
3/4 oz. Dubonnet
2 tsp. cherry brandy
2 tsp. orange juice

Cocktail; shake with ice, strain over ice.

NOSEBREAKER

Mafia dons enjoy this one.

1 oz. white crème de cacao
1 oz. green crème de menthe
1 oz. cherry brandy

Highball; pour, in order, over ice. Do not stir.

NOWHERE TO GO

1 1/2 oz. whiskey
1 1/2 oz. prune juice
1 oz. grapefruit juice

Old Fashioned; shake with ice, strain over ice.

OLD MAN

1 1/2 oz. bourbon
1 tbsp. rye
2 dashes Angostura bitters

Highball; shake with ice, strain over ice. Add lemon twist.

OLD MAN'S CASKET

1 1/2 oz. rye
1/2 oz. bourbon
2 dashes orange bitters

Highball; shake with ice, strain over ice. Add orange twist.

ORGANIC COCKTAIL

For all you macrobiotics out there.

1 1/2 oz. melon liqueur
1 oz. vodka
1/2 oz. green crème de menthe
1/2 oz. heavy cream

Old Fashioned; shake with ice, strain over ice.

PACEMAKER

1 1/2 oz. brandy
1 1/2 oz. whiskey
2 tbsp. banana liqueur

Old Fashioned; shake with ice, strain over ice. Add banana liqueur.

PACER

1 oz. tequila
1/2 oz. Drambuie
2 oz. grapefruit juice

Highball; pour over ice,
stir.

PEACH VELVET

1 1/2 oz. peach brandy
2 tbsp. white crème de
cacao
2 tbsp. heavy cream
1 tbsp. Kahlua
Sliced peaches
3 oz. crushed ice

Old Fashioned; blend at
high speed, pour.

PEG-LEG

1 oz. dark rum
1 oz. light rum
2 oz. cream of coconut

Highball; shake with ice,
strain over ice.

PENGUIN

1 1/4 oz. black cherry
brandy
1 1/4 oz. peppermint
schnapps
1/2 oz. club soda

Highball; pour over ice,
add club soda, stir gently.

PILEDRIVER

see BROWN OUT

PIT AND PENDULUM

Very Poe-ian.

2 oz. vodka
1 1/2 oz. Kahlua
1 oz. dark crème de
cacao

Old Fashioned; shake with
ice, strain over ice.

POLECAT

2 oz. tequila
1 tbsp. lime juice
2 tsp. crushed lemon
pulp

Cocktail; shake with ice,
strain over ice.

PRAIRIE DOG

2 oz. vodka
1/2 oz. tequila
2 tbsp. maraschino
liqueur
2 oz. grapefruit juice

Old Fashioned; shake with
ice, strain over ice. Add
maraschino liqueur.

PRESSED DUCK

2 oz. whiskey
1/2 oz. lemon juice
1/2 tsp. orange bitters

Old Fashioned; shake with
ice, strain over ice.

PRINCE VALIANT

1 1/2 oz. Southern Comfort
1/2 oz. scotch
1 tsp. cherry brandy
2 drops white crème de menthe

Old Fashioned; shake with ice, strain over ice. Float crème de menthe.

PURPLE COW

1 oz. blackberry brandy
1 oz. light cream
1 tsp. almond extract

Old Fashioned; shake with ice, strain over ice.

QUEEN BEE

1 oz. vodka
1 oz. light rum
1/2 oz. brandy
1 tbsp. honey
2 oz. orange juice

Old Fashioned; shake with ice, strain over ice.

QUEEN'S ELIXIR

1 1/4 oz. curaçao
1/2 oz. vodka
2 tbsp. grape juice
2 tbsp. cranberry juice
1 tsp. lemon juice

Old Fashioned; shake with ice, strain over ice.

RADAR RIDER

1 oz. gin
1 oz. vodka
1/2 oz. dry vermouth

Highball; shake with ice, strain over ice. Add lemon twist and 2 cocktail onions.

RAIL-RUNNER

1 1/2 oz. tequila
1 tbsp. lime juice
1 tbsp. lemon juice
1 tsp. grenadine
Pinch of salt

Old Fashioned; shake with ice, strain over ice. Add cherry.

RAVEN'S FEATHER

2 oz. Kahlua
1/2 oz. anisette
1 tbsp. vodka

Highball; shake with ice, strain over ice.

REDHEAD

2 oz. cherry brandy
1/2 oz. vodka
1 tbsp. grenadine

Old Fashioned; pour over ice, stir.

REDIRECT

2 oz. Southern Comfort
1/2 oz. sloe gin
1/2 oz. orange juice

Old Fashioned; shake with ice, strain over ice. Add lemon twist.

ROAD WARRIOR

For a different kind of Gibson.

1 oz. vodka
1/4 oz. Sambuca
1 tbsp. Kahlua
1 tbsp. white crème de cacao

Highball; shake with ice, strain over ice. Add cherry.

ROBBERY

also called ROBBER'S DELIGHT

2 oz. gin
1/2 oz. sloe gin
1 tbsp. curaçao
1 tsp. lemon juice

Old Fashioned; shake with ice, strain over ice.

ROCKY GREEN DRAGON

1 oz. gin
1 tbsp. cognac
1 tbsp. green Chartreuse

Old Fashioned; shake with ice, strain over ice.

ROMAN CANDLE

1 1/2 oz. gold rum
1 tbsp. lime juice
1 tbsp. lemon juice
1 tsp. apple brandy
1 tsp. 151-proof rum

Cocktail; shake with ice, strain. Float and ignite 151-proof rum.

RUSSIAN GAROTTE

2 oz. vodka
2 tbsp. curaçao
1 oz. grapefruit juice

Highball; shake with ice, strain over ice. Add cherry.

RUSSIAN ROULETTE

3/4 oz. Galliano
1/2 oz. banana brandy
1/2 oz. vodka
1/2 oz. orange juice
1 tbsp. lemon juice

Highball; shake with ice, strain over ice.

SANTIAGO SURPRISE

2 oz. light rum
1 oz. dark rum
3 drops grenadine

Old Fashioned; shake with ice, strain over ice. Add cherry.

SATCHEL CHARGE

2 oz. dry gin
1 oz. sloe gin
1/2 oz. dry vermouth
1 tbsp. curaçao
3 tbsp. grapefruit juice
2 drops grenadine

Highball; shake with ice, strain over ice. Add grenadine.

SEER-SUCKER

1 1/2 oz. dry gin
1 1/2 oz. sloe gin
1/2 oz. dry vermouth
2 tbsp. triple sec
1 tsp. orange bitters

Old Fashioned; shake with ice, strain over ice.

SLEDGEHAMMER

Mr. Gabriel's top selection.

2 1/2 oz. cognac
3 oz. orange juice
1 oz. grapefruit juice

Old Fashioned; shake with ice, strain over ice.

SOUTHERN BELLE

1 1/2 oz. bourbon
1 oz. heavy cream
1 tbsp. green crème de menthe
1 tbsp. white crème de cacao

Highball; shake with ice, strain. Add cherry.

SQUASHED FROG

1 1/2 oz. melon liqueur
1 oz. vodka
1/2 oz. crème de noyaux
2 oz. orange juice
1 tsp. grenadine
1 tsp. crushed cherries.

Collins; shake with ice, strain over ice. Stir in cherries. Float grenadine.

Use Midori for a MIDORI SQUASHED FROG.

STARFISH FRANKIE

1 oz. vodka
1 oz. sloe gin
2 tsp. green Chartreuse

Old Fashioned; shake with ice, strain over ice.

SUBMARINER

2 oz. vodka
1/2 oz. each light rum
  and spiced rum
1 tbsp. melon liqueur
1 tsp. lemon juice

Old Fashioned; shake with ice, strain over ice. Add lime twist.

SUBURBAN

1 oz. each whiskey and
  rum
2 tsp. port wine
2 dashes Angostura
  bitters
2 dashes orange bitters

Old Fashioned; shake with
ice, strain over ice.

TABOO

1 oz. vodka
1 oz. rum
2 tbsp. pineapple juice
2 tsp. lemon juice
3 drops sugar syrup
Crushed ice

Goblet; blend until
smooth. Garnish with
cherry, lemon slice, and
mint sprigs.

TAPEWORM

1 oz. tequila
1 oz. light rum
1/2 oz. lemon juice
1 tbsp. sloe gin
1 tbsp. grapefruit juice

Old Fashioned; shake with
ice, strain over ice.

TATTERED RAGS

1/2 oz. vodka
1/2 oz. rum
1/2 oz. whiskey
2 oz. pineapple juice
2 tbsp. light cream

Old Fashioned; pour over
ice, stir.

TESTER

2 oz. vodka
1 oz. tequila
1/2 oz. sweet vermouth
1 tbsp. curaçao
1 tsp. grenadine

Old Fashioned; shake with
ice, strain over ice. Add
cherry.

THIRD BASE

1 oz. gin
1/2 oz. sloe gin
1/2 oz. sweet vermouth
1 oz. orange juice

Old Fashioned; shake with
ice, strain over ice.

TORPEDO

2 oz. Calvados
1 tbsp. brandy
1 tsp. gin

Cocktail; shake with ice,
strain over ice.

ULYSSES

1 1/2 oz. cherry brandy
1 1/2 oz. dry vermouth

Old Fashioned; shake with
ice, strain over ice. Add
orange twist.

UNIMOG

2 oz. tequila
1 oz. brandy
2 tbsp. orange juice

Cocktail; shake with ice,
strain over ice.

UTTER CHAOS

1 oz. Frangelico
1 oz. Haagen-Däzs
  liqueur
2 oz. milk

Old Fashioned; pour over
ice, stir.

VELVET PEACH

see PEACH VELVET

VOODOO KINCADE

*The author's personal
favorite.*

1 1/2 oz. spiced rum
1 1/2 oz. dark rum
1 oz. Jamaican rum
2 oz. each pineapple,
  orange, and cranberry
  juice
1 tbsp. melon liqueur
1 tsp. cherry brandy
1 tsp. lemon juice

Big Old Fashioned; shake
with ice, strain over ice.
Add cherry, lime, and
lemon twist.

WAKE-UP CALL

1 1/2 oz. light rum
1/2 oz. whiskey
3 oz. orange juice
1 tbsp. grenadine

Old Fashioned; shake with
ice, strain over ice.

WESTERN OMELET

1 oz. brandy
1/2 oz. Grand Marnier
1/2 oz. dark rum
1/2 oz. sloe gin
1 tbsp. melon liqueur
1 oz. pineapple juice
1 oz. orange juice
1 oz. cranberry juice

Old Fashioned; shake with
ice, strain over ice.

WICKED NECTAR

2 oz. tequila
2 oz. whiskey
3 oz. mango nectar
1 oz. banana puree
1 tbsp. lime juice

Old Fashioned; shake with ice, strain over ice.

WITCH HAZEL

Doubles as a kitchen floor cleaner!

1 1/3 oz. gin
1 1/3 oz. vodka
1 1/3 oz. light rum
2 oz. grapefruit juice

Old Fashioned; shake with ice, strain over ice.

X-CELERATOR

2 oz. vodka
2 oz. celery juice
1 tbsp. lemon juice

Highball; pour over ice, stir.

YAK'S MILK

2 oz. Bailey's Irish Cream
1/2 oz. Kahlua
2 tbsp. spiced rum
1 oz. heavy cream

Old Fashioned; shake with ice, strain.

YOLANDA

1 oz. gin
3/4 oz. brandy
1/2 oz. sweet vermouth
1 tbsp. Pernod

Cocktail; pour, stir.

ZAPPED

1 1/2 oz. whiskey
1 oz. curaçao
2 tbsp. grapefruit juice

Cocktail; shake with ice, strain. Add cherry.

What do you call 1,000 Hollywood agents jumping out of an airplane?

> *Air pollution.*

What do you call 100 Hollywood agents buried up to their necks in sand?

> *Not enough sand.*

Why do Hollywood agents carry sludge in their back pockets?

> *Identification.*

What do you call 100 Hollywood agents sitting on a lawn?

> *Fertilizer.*

What's the difference between a bucket of sludge and a Hollywood agent?

> *The bucket.*

How do you get 1,000 Hollywood agents into the trunk of a Volkswagen Beetle?

> *Cuisinart.*

What's the best way to unload 100 Hollywood agents from the back of a truck?

> *Use a pitchfork.*

Why did the Hollywood agent cross the road?

> *He was stapled to the chicken.*

How many actors does it take to change a lightbulb?

> *Only one, as long as there's a director present.*

What do you call 1,000 Hollywood agents at the bottom of the ocean?

> *A good start.*

A Great White Shark came upon a Hollywood agent scuba diving on his day off. Why didn't he eat him?
  Professional courtesy.

The other day, a man came to my door and asked me if I wanted to buy a ticket to the Hollywood Agents Ball. I told him I didn't dance. He casually replied,
 "It's not a dance, it's a raffle."

What's the difference between a Hollywood agent and a catfish?
  One's a scum-sucking bottom dweller and the other's a fish.

What do you call a Hollywood agent who's convicted of three felonies?
  A rookie.

How do we know that all Hollywood agents are circumcised?
  Are you kidding? They take at least 10 percent off everything!

 A Jew, a Hindu, and a Hollywood agent were driving across the country when their car broke down late one night. After walking for miles, they came upon a small farm. After rousing the farmer from his slumber, they were granted permission to spend the night, but there was just one problem: the farmer's house only had two spare beds. One of the three men would have to spend the night in the barn.
 Being a kind and generous sort, the Jew volunteered, and off he went to sleep in the barn. The other two went to their beds. Less than twenty minutes later, there was a knock at the door. It was the Jew.
 "I am sorry to say that I cannot spend the night in the barn," he explained. "There is a pig in the barn and

my religion does not permit me to share the same roof with swine."

"Not to worry," said the Hindu. "I will sleep in the barn."

And off he went, while the Jew and the Hollywood agent retired to their beds. But not more than fifteen minutes later, there was another knock at the door. This time, it was the Hindu.

"I am sorry to complain, but I, too, cannot sleep in the barn," he explained. "There is a cow in the barn and my religious beliefs do not allow me to share the same roof with cattle."

"Not a problem," said the Hollywood agent. "I have very few morals and beliefs. I'll spend the night in the barn."

And off he went while the Jew and the Hindu retired to their beds. Less than five minutes later, there was another knock at the door. Unsure of what the problem could be, the Jew and the Hindu opened it slowly.

It was the pig and the cow.

I DON'T WANNA REMEMBER A THING!

In retrospect, maybe this section should have preceded the preceding section. After all, these are the drinks that can bring a person to the state of mind—and body—where they'll be asking themselves—kicking themselves is more like it—why in the heck they drank what they did. This section offers elixirs that will, and I strongly stress the word *will*, make you forget anything you did the night before. Of all the categories in this book, perhaps this one is best suited for the lawyers, politicians, and telemarketers of this world.

ACHIN' JOHNSON

Definitely something to forget.

1 oz. whiskey
1 oz. dark rum
1/4 oz. Grand Marnier
Orange juice

Collins; shake with ice, strain over ice, fill with orange juice. Orange garnish.

ALABAMA SHERIFF

1 oz. brandy
1/2 oz. curaçao
1/2 oz. lime juice
1 tsp. sugar

Old Fashioned; shake with ice, strain over ice. Add lemon twist.

ALICE IN WONDERLAND

1 oz. vodka
1 oz. tequila
1 oz. light rum
1 oz. gin
1 tsp. raspberry syrup

Old Fashioned; slowly pour for layered effect, add raspberry syrup.

ALIEN'S BLOOD

1 oz. vodka
1 oz. green crème de menthe
1/2 oz. blackberry brandy
1 tsp. lime juice

Highball; shake with ice, strain over ice, add lime juice.

APE SHAPE

1 oz. whiskey
1 oz. banana liqueur
1/2 oz. tequila
1/2 oz. gin
Pineapple juice
1 tbsp. cream of coconut

Collins; pour over ice, fill with juice, stir. Add cream of coconut. Add orange slice.

ARTILLERY

No, those aren't cannons that you hear—it's your head.

2 oz. gin
3/4 oz. sweet vermouth
2 dashes Angostura
  bitters

Old Fashioned; shake with ice, strain over ice. Add lemon twist.

ASPHALT SUCKER

1 oz. whiskey
1 oz. light or dark rum
1/2 oz. cherry brandy
Club soda

Highball; pour over ice, add soda, stir gently.

ASPIRIN SUBSTITUTE

Will definitely make the pain disappear.

1 oz. 151-proof rum
1 oz. vodka
1/2 oz. dry gin
Grapefruit juice

Old Fashioned, rim glass with salt; shake with ice, strain over ice.

ATOMIC BODYSLAM

Like joining the World Wrestling Federation!

1 oz. vodka
1 oz. gin
1 oz. dark rum
1 oz. blackberry brandy
Orange juice or
  grapefruit juice

Big Old Fashioned; shake with ice, strain over ice. Fill with juice.

AUTISTIC SAVANT

Worked for Rainman.

2 oz. scotch whiskey
1/2 oz. apricot brandy

Highball; pour over ice, stir.

B AND A TOMAHAWK

1 oz. Bailey's Irish Cream
1 oz. brandy
1/2 oz. sloe gin

Snifter; shake with ice, strain.

BALD PLUMBER

1 1/2 oz. whiskey
1 oz. Drambuie
Pineapple and prune juice

Old Fashioned; shake with ice, strain over ice. Fill with juices.

BANZAI RUNNER

2 oz. sake
2 oz. gin

Old Fashioned; pour over ice, stir.

BIG DADDY

1 oz. vodka
1 oz. tequila
1 oz. light rum
1 oz. whiskey
Ginger ale, 7-Up, or Sprite

Collins; pour over ice, fill with soda. Lemon or lime garnish.

BLACKOUT

2 oz. blackberry brandy
1 oz. bourbon
1 tbsp. lemon juice

Old Fashioned; shake with ice, pour over ice.

BLEEDING HEART

My tribute to the liberals.

2 oz. apple brandy
1 oz. light rum
1 tbsp. grenadine
1 tsp. lemon juice
1 tsp. 151-proof rum

Highball; pour over ice and stir, then float 151-proof rum.

BLUE SHARK

1 1/2 oz. tequila
1 1/2 oz. vodka
1/2 oz. blue curaçao

Old Fashioned; shake with ice, strain over ice.

BOMB SHELTER

2 1/2 oz. Irish whiskey
1 oz. sweet vermouth
2 dashes Angostura bitters

Highball; shake with ice, strain over ice.

BOOBY TRAP

Gets you when you least expect it.

1/2 oz. vodka
1/2 oz. gin
1/2 oz. light rum
1/2 oz. tequila
1 tsp. Grand Marnier
Orange and cranberry
  juice

Collins; shake with ice, strain over ice. Fill with juices. Float Grand Marnier on top.

BORDER-CROSSER

1 1/2 oz. tequila
1 1/2 oz. whiskey
2 tbsp. orange juice

Old Fashioned; shake with ice, strain over ice.

BULLET

2 oz. bourbon
2 oz. dry vermouth

Highball; pour over ice, stir. Add lemon twist.

CALAMITY JANE

1 oz. bourbon
1 oz. gin
1/2 oz. dry vermouth

Old Fashioned; shake with ice, pour over ice. Add lemon twist.

CAR CRASH

Another D.U.I. waiting to happen, so don't chance it.

1 oz. gin
1 oz. vodka
1/2 oz. whiskey
1/2 oz. tequila
1/2 oz. light rum
Orange, pineapple, and
  cranberry juice.

Goblet; shake with ice, pour over ice. Fill with juice. Add cherry, orange, and lime slices.

CHAMBER OF HORRORS

1 oz. whiskey
1 oz. cherry brandy
1/2 oz. lemon-flavored
  vodka

Highball; pour over ice, stir.

CHERRY-PICKER

1 oz. vodka
1 oz. cherry brandy
1/2 oz. gin

Old Fashioned; pour over ice, stir.

CITY SLICKER

1 1/2 oz. brandy
1 oz. curaçao

Snifter; shake with ice, strain over ice. Add lemon peel.

COCAINE SHOOTER

Tastes like a gummy-bear.

1 1/2 oz. vodka
1 oz. crème de noyaux
1/2 oz. amaretto
2 tbsp. grenadine

Old Fashioned; shake with ice, strain over ice.

CONEHEAD

You have successfully gnarfled the Garthog!

1 1/2 oz. light rum
1/2 oz. dark rum
1/2 oz. vodka
1 tbsp. apricot brandy

Old Fashioned; shake with ice, strain over ice. Add apricot brandy.

CONTINENTAL DIVIDE

1 oz. spiced rum
1 oz. green Chartreuse
1 tsp. lemon juice

Cocktail; shake with ice, strain.

CRIMSON TIDE

2 oz. gin
1/2 oz. vodka
1 oz. port wine
1 tsp. lemon juice
1 tsp. grenadine

Highball; shake with ice, strain over ice. Float port.

CRISS-CROSS

1/2 oz. vodka
1/2 oz. sloe gin
1 oz. whiskey
Pineapple juice

Collins; shake with ice, strain over ice. Fill with juice. Lemon and orange garnish.

D-TRAIN

No token necessary.

2 oz. tequila
2 oz. light rum
1 tsp. lemon juice

Old Fashioned; shake with ice, strain over ice.

DANCING LEPRECHAUN

2 oz. Irish Whiskey
1 oz. Drambuie
Pineapple juice
Ginger ale

Collins; pour over ice, fill with pineapple juice and ginger ale. Add lemon twist.

DELTA WARLORD

1 1/2 oz. whiskey
1 oz. Southern Comfort
2 tsp. lime juice
1 tsp. chocolate syrup

Old Fashioned; shake with ice, strain over ice.

DESTINY SPECIAL

1 oz. vodka
1/2 oz. sloe gin
1/2 oz. sweet vermouth
1/2 oz. tequila
1 tsp. lime juice
Club soda

Collins; pour over ice, fill with soda, stir. Top with cherry.

DEVILWATER

also called DEVIL'S RAIN

2 oz. vodka
1 oz. tequila
1/2 oz. light rum
Few dashes Angostura bitters
2 drops Tabasco sauce

Old Fashioned; shake with ice, strain over ice. Add Tabasco sauce.

DOUBLE-TRIGGER

1 oz. vodka
1 oz. tequila
2 oz. sweet vermouth
1/2 oz. orange juice

Highball; shake with ice, strain over ice. Add orange juice, stir.

DOUBLE-TROUBLE

1 1/2 oz. scotch
1 1/2 oz. Southern Comfort
2 drops grenadine

Highball; shake with ice, strain over ice.

DUMB BLONDE

Know any good "smart brunette" jokes?

1 1/2 oz. peach schnapps
1 1/2 oz. vodka
1/2 oz. apricot brandy

Old Fashioned; shake with ice, strain over ice.

EASTERN STORM

1 oz. dry sherry
1 1/2 oz. dry vermouth
1 tbsp. Grand Marnier
2 dashes orange bitters

Old Fashioned; shake with ice, strain over ice. Add orange bitters.

ECLIPSE

1 1/2 oz. sloe gin
1 1/2 oz. gin
1 tbsp. grenadine

Old Fashioned; shake with ice. Add grenadine. Strain over ice. Add orange twist and cherry.

EDGEWALKER

1 1/4 oz. tequila
1 1/4 oz. vodka
1/2 oz. orange juice
1 tsp. almond flavoring

Old Fashioned; shake with ice, strain over ice.

ELEPHANT KILLER

Barnum and Bailey outlawed this one.

1 1/4 oz. vodka
1 1/4 oz. tequila
1/2 oz. gin
1/2 oz. dry vermouth

Old Fashioned; shake with ice, strain over ice.

EVIL BASTARD

2 oz. whiskey
1 oz. brandy
1 tbsp. triple sec

Highball; shake with ice, strain over ice. Add lemon twist.

EYE OF THE STORM

2 oz. vodka
1 oz. dark rum
1 tbsp. scotch

Old Fashioned; shake with ice, strain over ice. Add scotch, lime slice.

FANATICAL CHILD

2 oz. Drambuie
1 oz. dark crème de cacao
1 oz. sweet vermouth
1 tbsp. anisette

Old Fashioned; shake with ice, strain over ice. Add lemon twist.

FIDDLESTICK

2 oz. bourbon
1 oz. sweet vermouth
1/2 oz. sloe gin

Old Fashioned; shake with ice, strain over ice.

FLAMETHROWER

Keep away from lighted matches!

1 oz. tequila
1 oz. gold rum
1/2 oz. lime juice
1 tbsp. grenadine
1 tbsp. 151-proof rum

Old Fashioned; shake with ice, strain over ice. Add 151-proof rum and ignite.

FLOODWATER

Don't mention this one in the Midwest.

1 1/2 oz. vodka
1 1/2 oz. light rum
1/2 oz. tequila
1 tsp. lime juice

Highball; shake with ice, strain over ice. Add lemon twist.

FLYING FORTRESS

1 oz. vodka
1 1/2 oz. cognac
1/2 oz. Cointreau
1/2 oz. anisette

Cocktail; pour and stir.

FOGCUTTER

1 1/2 oz. rum
1/2 oz. brandy
1/4 oz. gin
1 1/2 oz. orange juice

Highball; shake with ice, strain over ice. Add cherry.

FOGMAKER

2 oz. brandy
1 oz. bourbon
1/2 oz. sloe gin
Pineapple juice

Collins; pour over ice, fill with pineapple juice. Stir. Lime garnish.

FROZEN ZOMBIE

1 1/2 oz. gold rum
3 tsp. lime juice
1 tbsp. Jamaican rum
1 tbsp. light rum
1 tbsp. pineapple juice
1 tbsp. papaya juice
1 1/2 tsp. sugar syrup
1 tsp. 151-proof rum
Crushed ice

Collins; blend at high speed, strain. Pineapple wedge garnish.

FUR BATH

2 oz. tequila
1 oz. bourbon
Orange juice with pulp
1/2 tsp. grenadine

Old Fashioned; pour over ice, fill with orange juice, stir. Add grenadine.

GAS MASK

2 oz. gin
1 oz. dry vermouth
1/2 oz. triple sec
1 tbsp. lemon juice
1 tbsp. lime juice

Old Fashioned; shake with ice, strain over ice. Add lemon twist.

GATED DRIVE

1 oz. dark rum
1 oz. vodka
1/2 oz. amaretto
2 oz. pineapple juice
1 1/2 oz. cream of
  coconut

Old Fashioned; shake with
ice, strain over ice.

GLOVED ASSASSIN

1 oz. vodka
1 oz. bourbon
1 oz. scotch
1 tbsp. black cherry
  brandy

Old Fashioned; shake with
ice, strain over ice. Add
lemon twist.

GLOWLIGHT

2 oz. gin
1 oz. Drambuie
1/2 oz. tequila
1 tsp. grenadine
1/2 tsp. 151-proof rum
Club soda
2 cherries

Collins; pour over ice, fill
with soda. Add grenadine
and cherries. Float rum.

GOMER'S NECTAR

*Back home again in
Indiana.*

2 oz. whiskey
1 1/2 oz. sweet vermouth
Lemonade; preferably
  pink.

Collins; pour over ice, fill
with lemonade.

GREEN SNAKE

2 oz. green crème de
  menthe
1 oz. vodka
1 oz. blackberry brandy

Old Fashioned; pour over
ice, stir.

GUNSLINGER

2 1/2 oz. tequila
1/2 oz. lime juice
Orange juice
1 tsp. crème de noyaux

Old Fashioned; shake with
ice, strain over ice. Fill
with juice. Add crème de
noyaux.

HEART WARMER

*Instant cardiac resuscita-
tion.*

3 oz. cognac
1 egg yolk
Dash of paprika

Snifter; shake with ice,
strain over ice. Sprinkle
with paprika.

HIGHLIFE

1/2 oz. tequila
1/2 oz. dark rum
1/2 oz. light rum
1/2 oz. gin
Pear and/or mango nectar

Big Old Fashioned; shake
with ice, strain over ice.
Fill with nectar.

HOG-TIED

1 1/2 oz. bourbon
1/2 oz. rye
1/2 oz. sweet vermouth

Highball; shake with ice,
strain over ice.

HORNET

1 oz. sloe gin
1/2 oz. peppermint
  schnapps
Cola

Highball; pour over ice, fill
with cola. Add slice of
lime.

HOUSTON ROLLERBALL

*also called HOUSTON
SPECIAL and JONATHON E.*

1 oz. vodka
1 oz. bourbon
1 oz. sloe gin
Dash orange bitters

Old Fashioned; shake with
ice, strain over ice.

HUNTER'S COCKTAIL

1 1/2 oz. rye
1 tbsp. cherry brandy

Old Fashioned; pour over
ice, stir. Add cherry.

ICED COFFEE DEVASTATOR

1 1/2 oz. dark rum
1 oz. vodka
1 oz. gold rum
1 tsp. light cream
Iced coffee

Collins; pour over ice, fill
with iced coffee, stir.

In addition to the DEVAS-
TATOR, there are dozens of
Iced Coffee "specials"—
you could devote an entire
book to them. Virtually
anything can be mixed
with coffee.

ICEPICK

*Magnum and Orville's
buddies drink.*

2 oz. whiskey
1 oz. dark crème de
  cacao
1/2 oz. Sambuca

Highball; shake with ice,
strain over ice.

IGLOO MELTER

1 oz. whiskey
1 oz. scotch
1/2 oz. Drambuie
1 tsp. lemon juice
2 drops lime juice

Old Fashioned; shake with ice, strain over ice. Add lime juice.

IMPERIAL FIGHTER

1 1/2 oz. dry gin
1 1/2 oz. dry vermouth
2 tsp. sweet vermouth
1 tsp. lemon juice
2 dashes maraschino bitters
2 dashes Angostura bitters

Old Fashioned; shake with ice, strain over ice. Add lemon twist.

INCOME TAX FRAUD

1 oz. vodka
1 oz. sloe gin
1 tbsp. sweet vermouth
1 tbsp. grapefruit juice
2 dashes Angostura bitters

Old Fashioned; shake with ice, strain over ice.

IRISH COOLER

3 oz. Irish whiskey
Club soda

Highball; pour over ice, stir. Add lemon twist.

IRISH EYES ARE SMILING

S.C. and the author drink these at The Galway.

2 oz. green crème de menthe
1/2 oz. vodka
2 tbsp. Irish whiskey
2 oz. heavy cream

Old Fashioned; shake with ice, strain over ice.

JADED WAYS

1 1/2 oz. tequila
1 oz. white crème de menthe
1 tsp. sugar syrup
2 drops white crème de cacao
2 drops curaçao

Old Fashioned; shake with ice, strain over ice.

JASPER'S SPECIAL SAUCE

1 1/2 oz. bourbon
1/2 oz. Frangelico

Cocktail; shake with ice, strain over ice. Add lemon twist.

JET FUEL

2 oz. vodka
1 oz. gin
1/2 oz. tequila
1 tsp. grenadine
2 drops Tabasco sauce

Old Fashioned; shake with
ice, strain over ice.

JET-SETTER

1 1/2 oz. gin
1 oz. dry vermouth
1 oz. sweet vermouth
1 tsp. lime juice
1 tsp. grapefruit juice

Highball; shake with ice,
strain over ice. Add cherry.

JOHNSON

2 oz. vodka
1 oz. sloe gin
1/2 oz. curaçao

Old Fashioned; shake with
ice, strain over ice.

JONATHAN E.

see HOUSTON ROLLERBALL

JUDGE

1 1/2 oz. vodka
1 1/2 oz. tequila
1/2 oz. light rum
1 tsp. grenadine

Old Fashioned; shake with
ice, strain over ice. Add
lemon twist.

KISS-ASS BLASTER

*In layman's terms, a
twistin' triple.*

2 oz. vodka
1 oz. gin
1 oz. whiskey
1 oz. sloe gin
1 oz. dark rum
2 tbsp. lime juice
Orange and cranberry
  juice

Goblet; shake with ice,
strain over ice. Fill with
juices. (Serves 2)

KITCHEN SINK

Everything but...

1/2 oz. dark rum
1/2 oz. light rum
1/2 oz. spiced rum
1/2 oz. vodka
1/2 oz. gin
1/2 oz. tequila
1/2 oz. sweet vermouth
Pineapple, orange, and
  grapefruit juice

Collins; shake with ice,
strain over ice. Fill with
juices. Garnish with any
fruit.

KNUCKLE-BUSTER

*also called KNUCKLE-
DUSTER*

1 1/2 to 2 oz. scotch
1 oz. Drambuie
1 tsp. 151-proof rum

Old Fashioned; pour over
ice, stir.

LADYHAWK

1 1/2 oz. vodka
2 tbsp. white crème de
  cacao
1 tsp. light rum
1 oz. heavy cream

Old Fashioned; shake with
ice, strain over ice.

LADYKILLER

2 oz. whiskey
1/2 oz. vodka
1 tbsp. white crème de
  cacao

Old Fashioned; shake with
ice, strain over ice.

LASERADE

1 1/2 oz. sloe gin
1/2 oz. vodka
2 tbsp. grenadine
Lemonade

Collins; shake with ice,
strain over ice. Fill with
lemonade, leaving room to
add grenadine.

LESTER

*also called LESTER'S
COCKTAIL*

2 oz. bourbon
1/2 oz. sweet vermouth
1 tsp. lemon juice

Cocktail; shake with ice,
strain. Add lemon twist.

LOUDMOUTH

1 oz. brandy
1 oz. gin
1 tbsp. lemon juice

Old Fashioned; shake with
ice, strain over ice.

LOUDSPEAKER

1 oz. brandy
1 oz. gin
1 tbsp. lime juice

Old Fashioned; shake with
ice, strain over ice.

LOVER'S LEAP

2 oz. vodka
1/2 oz. bourbon
2 drops anisette

Old Fashioned; shake with
ice, strain over ice.

MALCONTENT

1 1/2 oz. Drambuie
1 oz. vodka
1 tbsp. lime juice
1 tsp. lemon juice
Grapefruit juice

Highball; pour over ice. Fill
with grapefruit juice, stir.

MATHEMATICIAN

2 oz. light rum
1 1/2 oz. dark rum
1/2 oz. tequila
2 oz. grapefruit juice

Old Fashioned; shake with ice, strain over ice.

MAYDAY

S.O.S.—Save Our Stomachs!

1 oz. whiskey
1 oz. Southern Comfort
2 dashes orange bitters

Old Fashioned; shake with ice, strain over ice.

MEXICO CITY

2 oz. light rum
1 1/2 oz. tequila
1 tbsp. orange juice

Old Fashioned; shake with ice, strain over ice.

MIND ERASER

Works better than a magnet on a floppy disk.

1 oz. vodka
1 oz. tequila
1/2 oz. light rum
1/2 oz. peppermint
  schnapps

Old Fashioned; shake with ice, strain over ice.

MIXED BLESSINGS

1/2 oz. gold rum
2 tbsp. crushed pineapple
2 tsp. 151-proof rum
2 drops lime juice
3 to 4 oz. pineapple juice
Crushed ice

Old Fashioned; blend and serve.

MORNING BREATH

1 oz. scotch
1 oz. brandy
1 tsp. blue curaçao
1 tbsp. orange juice
1 tbsp. grapefruit juice
2 dashes Angostura
  bitters

Old Fashioned; shake with ice, strain over ice.

MOTHER OF
THE YEAR

1 oz. apple brandy
1 oz. vodka
1 oz. tequila
1 oz. gin
Orange and cranberry
  juice

Collins; pour over ice, fill with juice, stir. Add 2 cherries.

NAIL IN THE COFFIN

1 1/2 oz. whiskey
1 1/2 oz. dry vermouth
1 tbsp. sweet vermouth
2 dashes Angostura
  bitters

Old Fashioned; shake with ice, strain over ice.

NAPALM BOMB

1 1/2 oz. Bailey's Irish
  Cream
1 1/2 oz. light rum
1/2 oz. cherry brandy

Highball; shake with ice, strain over ice.

NAVAHO

1 oz. whiskey
1/2 oz. bourbon
1/2 oz. tequila
2 dashes orange bitters
2 dashes maraschino
  bitters

Old Fashioned; shake with ice, strain over ice.

NEOPOLITAN HOTSHOT

1 oz. vodka
1 oz. Sambuca
1 tbsp. anisette
1 tbsp. spiced rum
2 drops Tabasco sauce

Old Fashioned; shake with ice, strain over ice. Add Tabasco sauce.

NEVERMIND

1 1/2 oz. Kahlua
1 oz. vodka
1 tbsp. Sambuca
1 tbsp. heavy cream

Highball; shake with ice, strain over ice. Gently add cream. Do not stir.

NEVER-NEVER LAND

For the Peter Pan—or Tinkerbell—in all of us.

2 oz. dark rum
2 oz. light rum
1 1/2 oz. gin
1 1/2 oz. sweet ver-
  mouth
1 oz. sloe gin
1 oz. lemon-flavored
  vodka
1 oz. tequila
Pineapple, orange, and
  cranberry juice

Goblet; shake with ice, strain over ice. Fill with juice. Add lemon wedge. (Serves 3)

NIGHT

1 1/2 oz. dark rum
1 1/2 oz. blackberry
  brandy

Cocktail; shake with ice, strain over ice. Add lemon or orange twist.

NORTHERN EXPRESS

1 oz. Canadian whiskey
1 oz. dry vermouth
1 oz. Cordial Medoc

Old Fashioned; shake with ice, strain over ice. Add cherry.

NOSEDIVE

1 oz. tequila
1 oz. sloe gin
1 tbsp. amaretto
1 tbsp. port wine

Cocktail; shake with ice, strain over ice.

OCTOPUS

Don't *try this one alone.*

2 oz. brandy
2 oz. vodka
2 oz. sloe gin
2 oz. whiskey
2 tbsp. lemon juice
2 tbsp. lime juice
Orange and pineapple
  juice
Crushed ice

Goblet or *mug;* blend at low speed, pour. (Serves 4)

O'MALLEY

2 oz. Irish whiskey
1 tbsp. lemon juice
1 tbsp. green crème de
  menthe

Old Fashioned; shake with ice, strain over ice.

ORCHID

2 oz. brandy
1 oz. apricot brandy
1 tbsp. grenadine

Old Fashioned; pour over ice, stir.

OSTRICH NECK

2 oz. gin
1 oz. light rum
1 tbsp. curaçao
1 egg white

Old Fashioned; shake with ice, strain over ice.

PADDY-WAGON

2 oz. Irish whiskey
1 1/2 oz. sweet vermouth
2 dashes Angostura
  bitters

Old Fashioned; shake with ice, strain over ice.

PALADIN

2 oz. dark rum
1 oz. spiced rum
1/2 oz. Galliano
1 1/2 oz. pineapple juice

Old Fashioned; shake with ice, strain over ice.

PARADISE LOST

2 oz. vodka
1 oz. cherry brandy
2 oz. pineapple juice

Old Fashioned; shake with ice, strain over ice.

PICASSO

2 oz. cognac
2 tsp. Dubonnet
2 tsp. lime juice
1 tsp. sugar syrup

Old Fashioned; shake with ice, strain over ice. Add orange twist.

PIRATE'S GROG

2 oz. light rum
1 oz. spiced rum
2 tbsp. amaretto
2 tbsp. grenadine
1 tsp. lime juice
1 tsp. lemon juice

Old Fashioned; shake with ice, strain over ice. Add lemon twist.

POKER FACE

2 oz. vodka
1 oz. sloe gin
1 tbsp. lemon juice

Old Fashioned; shake with ice, strain over ice.

PRISONER'S PUNCH

Sure beats that root beer in the 111th Precinct.

2 oz. bourbon
2 oz. vodka
1/2 oz. dark rum
2 tbsp. grapefruit juice
1 tbsp. prune juice

Old Fashioned; pour over ice, stir.

QUADRAPLEGIC

1 oz. brandy
1 oz. rum
1 oz. vodka
1 oz. gin
1 oz. orange juice
1 oz. pineapple juice
2 tbsp. lime juice
1 tbsp. lemon juice

Big Old Fashioned; shake with ice, strain over ice. Add 4 cherries.

RAY-GUN

An Independence Day crowd favorite.

1 oz. gin
1/2 oz. orange curaçao
1/2 oz. melon liqueur
1 tsp. lemon juice
2 drops lime juice
1/2 tsp. 151-proof rum

Highball; shake with ice, strain over ice. Float 151-proof rum.

REEF-WALKER

2 oz. gold rum
1/2 oz. Malibu rum
1 oz. pineapple juice

Old Fashioned; shake with
ice, strain over ice. Add
pineapple slice.

ROYAL COCKTAIL

1 1/2 oz. Canadian
  whiskey
1/2 oz. brandy
2 tbsp. lemon juice
2 dashes orange bitters

Highball; shake with ice,
strain over ice.

RYE AND DRY

2 oz. dry vermouth
1 oz. rye
2 dashes orange bitters

Old Fashioned; shake with
ice, strain over ice.

SCAMMER

also called SCHEMER

1 oz. Jamaican rum
1/4 to 1/2 oz. lemon
  juice
1 tsp. 151-proof rum

Cocktail; shake with ice,
strain. Add 151-proof rum.
Chill.

SCARLET'S DANCE

1 oz. bourbon
1 oz. rye
2 tbsp. grenadine
2 tbsp. grapefruit juice
1 tsp. Tia Maria

Old Fashioned; shake with
ice, strain over ice.

SCATTERBRAIN

2 oz. vodka
1/2 oz. tequila
1/2 oz. grapefruit juice
2 tbsp. grenadine
1 tsp. lime juice

Old Fashioned; shake with
ice, strain over ice.

SEVEN DEADLY SINS

1/2 oz. vodka
1/2 oz. gin
1/2 oz. tequila
1/2 oz. light rum
1/2 oz. dark rum
1/2 oz. dry vermouth
1/2 oz. sweet vermouth
2 tbsp. grenadine
1 tsp. lemon or lime
  juice
Cola

Collins; pour over ice,
fill with cola, stir. Add
7 cherries.

SLEEPER

Woody's choice.

4 oz. red wine
1 tbsp. curaçao
1 tbsp. brandy

Old Fashioned; pour over ice, stir gently.

SLEEPING BEAUTY

2 1/2 oz. vodka
1/2 oz. dry gin
1 tbsp. grenadine
1 tsp. lemon juice

Old Fashioned; shake with ice, strain over ice. Add cherry.

STAR-GAZER

2 oz. brandy
1 oz. bourbon
1 tbsp. lemon juice
1 tbsp. pineapple juice

Old Fashioned; shake with ice, strain over ice. Add cherry.

STONEFISH

This one really stings!

2 oz. tequila
1 oz. whiskey
1 oz. sweet vermouth
1/2 oz. brandy
3 oz. cranberry juice

Old Fashioned; shake with ice, strain over ice.

TAIL 'O THE DOG

2 oz. tequila
1 tbsp. 151-proof rum
2 oz. grapefruit juice

Highball; pour over ice, stir. Add 151-proof rum.

TASK-MASTER

1 1/2 oz. vodka
1/2 oz. gin
1/2 oz. sloe gin
1 oz. cranberry juice
1 tbsp. grape juice
2 dashes maraschino
  bitters

Old Fashioned; shake with ice, strain over ice.

TAXI DRIVER

2 oz. bourbon or rye
2 oz. orange juice
1 tbsp. dry gin

Highball; pour over ice, stir. Add gin.

TENNESSEE EXPRESS

1 3/4 oz. rye
1 3/4 oz. brandy
2 tsp. maraschino liqueur
2 dashes green crème de
  menthe

Old Fashioned; shake with ice, strain over ice.

THIRD DEGREE

1 oz. vodka
1 oz. brandy
1 egg yolk

Snifter; shake with ice, strain over ice.

TIGER SHARK

2 oz. gin
1/2 oz. sloe gin
1/2 oz. sweet vermouth
1 tbsp. apple brandy
1 tbsp. cherry brandy

Old Fashioned; pour over ice, stir. Add apple brandy. Add cherry brandy.

TWELVE GAUGE

1 1/2 oz. tequila
1 oz. sloe gin
1 oz. sweet vermouth
2 oz. grapefruit juice

Old Fashioned; shake with ice, strain over ice.

TWO-TO-GO

2 oz. whiskey
2 oz. dark rum
2 oz. orange juice
2 tsp. grenadine

Old Fashioned; shake with ice, strain over ice.

VAMPIRE'S KISS

2 oz. vodka
1/2 oz. dry gin
1/2 oz. dry vermouth
1 tbsp. tequila
Pinch of salt
2 oz. tomato juice

Old Fashioned; shake with ice, strain over ice.

VERA

Ask Norm about this one.

2 oz. scotch
1 tbsp. Drambuie
1 tbsp. lemon juice
1 tsp. lime juice
1/2 tsp. sugar syrup

Old Fashioned; shake with ice, strain over ice.

WABASH

1/2 oz. gin
1 oz. lemon juice
1 tbsp. 151-proof rum

Cocktail; pour over ice, stir. Add lemon twist.

WASP ATTACK

The silent majority strikes back.

2 oz. Southern Comfort
1/2 oz. Drambuie
1 tbsp. pineapple juice
1 tbsp. grapefruit juice

Old Fashioned; shake with ice, strain over ice.

WATER DRAGON

2 oz. dry vermouth
1/2 oz. gin
1 tbsp. sweet vermouth
1 tbsp. vodka
2 tsp. lime juice
2 tsp. lemon juice

Highball; shake with ice, strain over ice.

WHITE WATER

Ms. Hillary, your drink is served.

3 oz. vodka
1 tbsp. dry vermouth
1 tbsp. lemon juice
Club soda

Collins; pour over ice, fill with soda, stir. Add lime twist.

WIDOWMAKER

2 oz. bourbon
1 oz. Drambuie
1/2 oz. scotch
1 oz. lemon juice
1 oz. orange juice

Old Fashioned; shake with ice, strain over ice.

X-RAY EYES

1 1/2 oz. vodka
1/2 oz. dry gin
1/2 oz. triple sec
2 oz. tomato juice

Old Fashioned; shake with ice, strain over ice. Add lemon slice.

YACHTSMAN'S PROVERB

1 oz. dark rum
1 oz. Jamaican rum
2 oz. cream of coconut
1 oz. pineapple juice
Crushed ice

Goblet; blend until smooth. Add cherry.

YO-YO

1 oz. dark rum
1 oz. light rum
2 oz. apple juice

Highball; pour over ice, stir.

YOZMERIDIAN

2 oz. brandy
1 tbsp. whiskey
1 tbsp. Kahlua
1 tsp. 151-proof rum

Snifter; pour over ice, stir lightly.

FIGHT NIGHT IN THE VALLEY

*Mixologists are no strangers to bar fights. And, yes,
I've seen a few good brawls during my bartending
tenure. Truth is, some nights when it's slow, you'd
much rather see a few drunks slug it out than pour
a half-dozen drinks and make a lousy $5 in tips. But
while tending bar one evening at a small, hole-in-the-
wall tavern in the San Fernando Valley, I wound up
with a ringside seat to the one barroom altercation
that stands out far above all the others I've witnessed.
It happened like this:*

*It seems a well-known actor, famous for his numer-
ous martial arts action films, chose this particular
night and this particular pub to drink and carouse with
a few of his friends. (For the record, I tried to get him
to sample one of my "famous" concoctions, but he and
his group were sticking to beer—quite a few, I might
add.) Anyway, after about an hour—and a half-dozen
pitchers—this famous celeb got antsy and started
jumping around with his buddies, pretending the bar
was his dojo, and practicing some of his kicks, punches, and other martial arts maneuvers. Despite being
asked to "take it easy" by the bouncers—celebs were
given a lot of latitude as their presence was deemed
"good for business"—his wild antics continued. And
intensified. It wasn't long before the famous actor got
really out of hand and challenged anyone in the bar—
anyone who "had the guts"—to a fight.*

*Sure enough, another patron—a plain, regular guy,
referred to as a "nobody" in Hollywood-speak—accept-
ed the challenge. Now, the challenger was not little by*

any means. Standing about 6'3", I guessed him to weigh around 220 pounds—all muscle.

So the movie star, who shall remain nameless—this isn't The Enquirer—walked over to his soon-to-be combatant and smiled. He said something to the effect of "You really think you can take me, huh?" and, before the reply, backed up a few paces and began demonstrating his considerable skill: aerial kicks, spinning punches, table jumps, etc., etc., etc.

While the movie star continued his drunken spectacle, the bouncers walked over to me for advice on how to handle the situation. (When the owner or the manager wasn't in—which, sadly, they weren't—the mixologist captained the ship.) I just shrugged. Man, I didn't have a clue. But, as of yet, no actual punches had been thrown, no damage had been done—except for a few broken bottles that the celeb had broken with his hands—and every person present, bouncers and bartender alike, was curious as to what the outcome would be.

Finally, after a dazzling, five-minute cavalcade of shadow fighting, the celeb strutted over to where his challenger stood, folded his arms across his chest and, in a voice dripping with cockiness, said, "Still think you can take me?"

The big guy smiled sheepishly, shrugged, looked over at the table where his friends sat, and quickly decked the movie star with a blow to the chin, dropping him smack onto his behind.

The celeb looked up at his "challenger," nodded respectfully, and fell backward, out cold.

His friends scraped the celebrity off the floor and hauled him out. The "winner" quietly went back to his table, finished his drink, and left with his party. In the *interest of all concerned, the bouncers and I agreed to sweep the matter under the bar mat and say no more about it. The customers, barely sure of what they had witnessed, were given a round on the house and seemed very satisfied.*

YOU DON'T EXPECT ME TO DRINK THAT, DO YOU?

Herein are the drinks that—sober—you would most assuredly avoid. Every now and then, during my tenure as a bartender, after mixing and pouring one of these famous "homegrown" potions for some "lucky" new customer, the chapter title is the response I would receive. Whether you choose to imbibe or not is completely up to you. But for the record, some of these concoctions are really good. It's getting past the name that's tough. Enjoy!

AIRHEAD

Let's see, two plus two is, uh...

1 oz. vodka
1 oz. sloe gin
1 tbsp. Kahlua
Club soda

Collins; pour over ice, fill with soda. Cherry garnish.

ALIEN

Highly recommended for close *encounters.*

1 1/2 oz. vodka
1/2 oz. whiskey
Grapefruit juice
3 olives

Big Old Fashioned; pour over ice, fill with grapefruit juice, stir. Add olives.

APACHE FIREWATER

2 oz. vodka
1/2 oz. 151-proof rum
2 oz. club soda
3 to 4 drops Tabasco sauce

Highball; pour over ice, add soda, stir. Top with Tabasco sauce.

APPENDICITIS

6 oz. gin
1 oz. dry vermouth
1 tbsp. grenadine
1 egg

Goblet; shake with ice, strain over ice. Serves two.

APPETITE SUPPRESSANT

Bulimia in a glass.

1 1/2 oz. dark crème de cacao
1 oz. dark rum
1/2 oz. heavy cream
1 tbsp. chocolate syrup
1 cup coffee

Hot Mug; pour hot coffee, then add ingredients.

ASS-KICKER

1 1/2 oz. vodka
1/2 oz. gin
1/2 oz. vermouth
Cranberry juice

Collins; pour over ice, fill with cranberry juice, stir. Lime garnish.

ATOMIC NECTAR

1 1/2 dark rum
1 oz. sweet vermouth
1/2 oz. dry gin

Highball; pour over ice, stir.

AXEHANDLE

2 oz. single-malt scotch
1 oz. dry vermouth
2 dashes Angostura bitters

Highball; shake with ice, strain over ice.

BABY GODZILLA

1 1/2 oz. light rum
1 oz. dark rum
1/2 oz. crème de noyaux

Highball; shake with ice, strain over ice.

BIG JOHNSON

You figure it out.

2 oz. vodka
2 oz. each light and dark rum
Orange and cranberry juice
1 banana, unpeeled

Big Old Fashioned; shake with ice, strain over ice. Fill with juice. Add banana. (Serves 2)

BLITZKRIEG

1 oz. Jagermeister
1/2 oz. gin
1/2 oz. dry vermouth
Club soda

Highball; pour over ice, fill with soda.

BLUE SQUID

1 1/2 oz. blue curaçao
1 oz. light rum
2 tbsp. white crème de cacao
1 tsp. cream

Old Fashioned; shake with ice, strain over ice.

BRAIN HEMORRHAGE

also called SIMON'S BRAIN

1 oz. each vodka, gin,
  and tequila
1 tsp. Bailey's Irish
  cream
2 drops grenadine
1 olive

Old Fashioned; shake
"whites" with ice, strain,
add olive, Bailey's, and
grenadine.

BUBBLE-BURSTER

2 oz. gin
1 oz. sloe gin
3 tbsp. lemon juice

Old Fashioned; shake with
ice, strain over ice.

CEMENT MIXER

*An excellent "prank"
drink.*

1 oz. Bailey's Irish Cream
1/2 tsp. lime juice

Shot Glass; pour Bailey's,
add lime juice. Bailey's
should begin to curdle.

CODE BREAKER

2 oz. dry gin
1 oz. dark crème de
  cacao
1/2 tsp. heavy cream

Old Fashioned; pour over
ice, do not stir. Add heavy
cream.

COVEN OF WITCHES

*also called WITCHES'
BREW*

1 1/2 oz. vodka
1 1/2 oz. dark rum
1/2 oz. Jagermeister

Old Fashioned; pour over
ice, stir. Add Jagermeister
last.

CREEPSHOW

1 oz. vodka
1 1/2 oz. green crème de
  menthe
2 tbsp. heavy cream
1 tsp. cherry brandy

Highball; shake with ice,
strain over ice. Add cherry
brandy.

DIRTY DIAPER

1 1/2 oz. Jagermeister
1 1/2 oz. tequila
1/2 tsp. light cream or
  milk

Cocktail; shake with ice,
strain. Add cream.

DRACULA'S BRIDE

1 oz. vodka
2 oz. cherry brandy
1/2 oz. sloe gin
Pinch of salt

Old Fashioned; shake with ice, strain over ice. Add salt.

DUNDEE

1 oz. gin
2 tbsp. scotch
2 tsp. Drambuie
1 tsp. lemon juice

Old Fashioned; shake with ice, strain over ice. Cherry garnish.

EGGFLOWER SOUP

3 oz. vodka
3 tsp. apricot brandy

Goblet or *Snifter;* pour vodka over ice, gently add brandy.

ELEPHANT'S BREATH

2 oz. scotch
3/4 oz. dry vermouth
2 dashes Angostura bitters
1 tsp. pineapple juice

Old Fashioned; shake with ice, strain over ice.

EMERALD ISLE

2 oz. dry gin
1 tsp. green crème de menthe
2 dashes Angostura bitters

Old Fashioned; shake with ice, strain over ice.

FALL OF THE GOOD ANGEL

Everyone's bad now and then.

2 oz. lemon-flavored vodka
2 oz. gold rum
2 dashes green Chartreuse
Dash orange bitters

Old Fashioned; shake with ice, strain over ice. Add cherry.

FESTERING BOIL

1 1/2 oz. Jagermeister
1/2 oz. dry gin
1/2 oz. vodka
2 cocktail onions

Highball; pour over ice, stir. Add onions.

FIG-LEAF FLIP

1 1/2 oz. sweet vermouth
1 oz. light rum
1 1/2 tbsp. lime juice
2 dashes Angostura
  bitters

Old Fashioned; shake with
ice, strain over ice.

FLAT GRASSHOPPER

1 oz. tequila
2 tsp. green crème de
  menthe
2 tsp. white crème de
  menthe
1 tsp. cherry brandy

Old Fashioned; shake with
ice, strain over ice.

FOAMING DOG

2 oz. vodka
1 oz. tequila
Grapefruit juice
Club soda
Pinch of baking soda

Goblet; shake with ice,
strain. Top with club soda.
Stir in baking soda.

FREDDY'S REVENGE

1 1/2 oz. vodka
1 oz. cherry brandy
1 oz. green crème de
  menthe

Old Fashioned; shake with
ice, strain over ice.

FUDGEPACKER

1 1/2 oz. dark crème de
  cacao
1 oz. vodka
1/2 oz. white crème de
  cacao
1/2 oz. chocolate syrup
1 tbsp. Bailey's Irish
  Cream

Old Fashioned; shake with
ice, strain over ice.

GANGRENE

2 oz. green crème de
  menthe
1 1/2 oz. vodka
1/2 oz. tequila
1 tbsp. blackberry brandy

Old Fashioned; shake with
ice, strain over ice.

GASSER

1 1/2 oz. scotch
1 oz. Drambuie
1 tbsp. sweet vermouth
2 dashes orange bitters

Old Fashioned; shake with
ice, strain over ice. Add
orange twist.

GATES OF HELL

2 oz. vodka
1 1/2 oz. gold rum
1 oz. apple brandy
2 drops Tabasco sauce

Highball; shake with ice,
strain over ice. Add
Tabasco sauce.

GOAT'S MILK

1 oz. dark rum
1 oz. tequila
2 oz. cream of coconut

Old Fashioned; shake with ice, strain over ice.

GODZILLA

Where's Megalon when you need him?

3 oz. light rum
2 oz. dark rum
1 oz. crème de noyaux

Goblet; shake with ice, strain over ice.

GORILLA SWEAT

2 oz. tequila
1 tsp. melted butter
1/2 tsp. sugar
Boiling water
Pinch of nutmeg

Old Fashioned; pour, add boiling water and butter, stir. Sprinkle nutmeg.

GREEN DRAGON

1 1/2 oz. gin
1 oz. green crème de menthe
2 tsp. lemon juice
1 tsp. white crème de cacao
2 dashes orange bitters

Old Fashioned; shake with ice, strain over ice.

GREEN HORNET

2 oz. vodka
2 oz. green crème de menthe
1/2 oz. light rum
1 tsp. lemon juice
1 tsp. lime juice

Old Fashioned; shake with ice, strain over ice.

HACKER

1 1/4 oz. tequila
1 oz. bourbon
1 tbsp. sugar syrup
Orange juice

Big Old Fashioned; pour over ice, fill with orange juice, stir. Add cherry.

HARD LUCK JOE

1 1/2 oz. scotch
1 oz. sweet vermouth
1 tsp. lemon juice
Dash of Angostura bitters

Old Fashioned; shake with ice, strain over ice.

HAZARDOUS WASTE

1 1/2 oz. green crème de menthe
1 oz. Jagermeister
1/4 to 1/2 oz. vodka or tequila
Pinch brown sugar
Crushed lemon and cherries

Cocktail; shake with ice, strain.

HERPETOLOGIST'S DREAM

2 1/2 oz. whiskey
1/2 oz. dark rum
1 tbsp. dry vermouth
Grapefruit juice

Collins; pour over ice, fill with grapefruit juice, stir.

HOLLOWPOINT COCKTAIL

This one will kill you!

3 oz. tequila
1 oz. gin
1 oz. sloe gin
1 oz. orange juice
1 tsp. lime juice
1 tsp. lemon juice
7-Up or Sprite

Goblet; shake with ice, strain over ice, fill with 7-Up. Add lemon and cherry.

HONEYMOON'S OVER

1 1/2 oz. tequila
1 1/2 oz. gin
1/2 oz. sweet vermouth
1 tbsp. lime juice
1 tsp. crushed lime pulp
1 tsp. grapefruit juice
2 drops grenadine

Old Fashioned; shake with ice, strain over ice. Add grenadine.

ICK

1 oz. tequila
1 oz. vodka
1/2 oz. light rum
2 tsp. lemon juice
Dash Angostura bitters

Cocktail; shake with ice, strain over ice.

INJUN ALE

1 oz. whiskey
2 drops Tabasco sauce
Cold beer

Beer Mug; pour whiskey, fill with beer, stir. Add Tabasco sauce.

ISLE OF PAIN

2 oz. tequila
1 oz. vodka
1/2 oz. gin
1 tbsp. grapefruit juice
1 tsp. lime juice

Highball; shake with ice, strain over ice. Add lime juice.

JAIL JUICE

Created at the 111th Precinct!

2 oz. vodka
2 oz. tequila
Pineapple, orange, and
    cranberry juice

Collins; pour over ice, fill
with juice, stir.

JERSEY LIGHTNING

2 1/2 oz. apple brandy
2 dashes Angostura bit-
    ters
Pinch of sugar

Old Fashioned; shake with
ice, strain over ice.

JIZZ

The *drink of the adult
film industry.*

2 oz. Bailey's Irish Cream
1/2 oz. vodka
1 tbsp. white crème de
    cacao
Pinch of salt
Milk
Splash of soda

Highball; pour over ice, fill
with milk. Add splash of
soda.

JOCK'S STRAP

*If you can't be an
athlete, be an athletic
supporter.*

1 oz. tequila
1 oz. bourbon
1 tsp. lime juice

Cocktail; shake with ice,
strain over ice. Add lime
juice.

JUNK

1 oz. vodka
1/2 oz. light rum
1/2 oz. gin
1/2 oz. tequila
1 tbsp. sloe gin
1 tbsp. brandy
1 tsp. lemon juice
Orange juice, pineapple
    juice, and cranberry
    juice

Big Old Fashioned; shake
with ice, strain over ice.
Fill with juices. Add various fruits.

KAHLUA TOREADOR

2 oz. brandy
1 oz. Kahlua
1 egg white

Old Fashioned; shake with
ice, strain over ice

KISS OF DEATH

2 oz. bourbon
1 oz. rye
1 oz. brandy
1 oz. orange juice
1 tbsp. grenadine

Old Fashioned; shake with ice, strain over ice. Add 2 cherries.

KRYPTONITE

Even defeats Superman.

2 oz. peppermint
  schnapps
1 oz. vodka
1 oz. melon liqueur
1 tsp. green or yellow
  Chartreuse

Old Fashioned; shake with ice, strain over ice.

KURD

1 1/2 oz. scotch
1 oz. port wine
1 oz. lemon-flavored
  vodka

Old Fashioned; pour over ice, stir.

LAB EXPERIMENT

What else would you call it?

2 oz. vodka
2 oz. gin
2 oz. sweet vermouth
1 oz. dry vermouth
1 oz. melon liqueur
1 oz. cherry brandy
Orange and cranberry
  juice
2 tbsp. 151-proof rum

Goblet; shake with ice, strain over ice. Add 151-proof rum. (Serves 2)

LAVA

2 oz. vodka
1 oz. cherry brandy
1 oz. heavy cream
2 drops Tabasco sauce

Old Fashioned; shake with ice, strain over ice. Add Tabasco sauce.

LEPRECHAUN'S WISH

After all, turnabout is fair play.

1 1/2 oz. Irish whiskey
1 1/2 oz. Southern
  Comfort

Highball; shake with ice, strain over ice. Add cherry.

LOCOMOTIVE

1 1/2 oz. whiskey
1 oz. scotch
2 oz. pineapple juice
1/2 oz. prune juice

Old Fashioned; shake with
ice, strain over ice. Add
cherry.

LONDON FOG

1 tbsp. white crème de
  menthe
1 tbsp. anisette
2 dashes Angostura bit-
  ters

Cocktail; pour over ice,
stir, strain.

LURCH

You rang?

2 oz. tequila
1/2 oz. grapefruit juice
1 tsp. lime juice
1 tsp. lemon juice
1 tsp. sugar syrup

Highball; shake with ice,
strain over ice.

MEDIEVAL SPECIAL

1 oz. port wine
1 oz. apricot brandy
1 oz. brandy
1/2 tsp. maraschino
  bitters

Old Fashioned; shake with
ice, strain over ice.

MIND BOGGLER

2 oz. gin
1 oz. sweet vermouth
1/2 oz. sloe gin
1/2 oz. dry vermouth
1 tsp. lemon juice

Old Fashioned; shake with
ice, strain over ice.

MIXED GREENS

1 1/2 oz. melon liqueur
1 1/2 oz. green crème de
  menthe
1/4 oz. vodka
1 tbsp. lime juice

Old Fashioned; shake with
ice, strain over ice. Add
lime slice.

MONKEY GLANDS

*Paints a pleasant picture,
don't you think?*

2 oz. gin
1 tbsp. sloe gin
1 tsp. dry vermouth
2 drops grenadine

Old Fashioned; shake with
ice, strain over ice.

MUDSUCKER

1 oz. Kahlua
1 oz. dark rum
1/2 oz. dark crème de
  cacao
1 tbsp. chocolate syrup

Old Fashioned; shake with
ice, strain over ice.

MURDER JUICE

2 oz. vodka
1/2 oz. light rum
1/2 oz. tequila
Cranberry juice

Collins; pour over ice, fill with cranberry juice, stir. Add lemon slice.

NECROPHILIAC'S DREAM

1 oz. light rum
1 oz. lime-flavored vodka
1 oz. white crème de cacao
1 tbsp. anisette

Old Fashioned; shake with ice, strain over ice.

NAPALM

2 oz. whiskey
1/2 oz. vodka
2 tbsp. 151-proof rum
Crushed ice

Old Fashioned; pour over crushed ice. Do not stir. Add 151-proof rum.

NIGHTSHADE

1 1/2 oz. Jagermeister
1 oz. tequila
1/2 oz. dry gin

Old Fashioned; pour over ice. Do not stir.

I'LL PICK IT OUT

It was during my first week in Los Angeles, and one of my first bartending jobs, that I learned a very important lesson: never get drunk with your colleagues. Either let them get drunk, or if they're going to stay sober, then you can get drunk, but don't all of you get drunk. Here's why:

My fourth night in L.A., my second night on the job, and I'm still looking for a place to live. One of the other bartenders I was working with, her name was Karen, was letting me crash with her for a few nights—I knew her from New York—until I found the perfect place of my own. However, I was new to L.A.

and, stupid me, I didn't know her address. (Yes, I probably should have written it down somewhere, but hindsight will kill you!) Every time I had been at her place, it was with her.

Anyway, we closed the bar, slammed a few (dozen) with the club's owner and, realizing we were in no condition to drive, called a taxi. When the cab arrived, we piled in.

"Where to?" asked the cabby.

A sensible question. I looked at her. But she looked at me.

"Where do you live?" I asked.

"I, uh, forgot," she replied.

So, after about a minute of clueless thinking, she leaned between the cab's open, sliding plastic partition and said to the cabby, "Just start driving. I'll pick it out."

Sure enough, roughly ninety minutes and $63 later, she did!

NIGHTSHADOW

1 1/2 oz. bourbon
2 tsp. sweet vermouth
2 tsp. orange juice
2 drops yellow Chartreuse

Cocktail; shake with ice, strain over ice. Add lemon slice.

NILE WATER

2 oz. dry gin
1 oz. dry vermouth
1 tbsp. lime juice
1 tsp. crushed lemon
   pulp
Club soda

Old Fashioned; shake with ice, strain over ice. Add splash of soda. Add lemon pulp.

OGRE

1 1/2 oz. tequila
1 oz. vodka
1/2 oz. triple sec
1 oz. each orange and
  grapefruit juice

Old Fashioned; shake with
ice, strain over ice.

ORGAN GRINDER

1 oz. dark rum
1 oz. light rum
1 oz. whiskey
1 tbsp. white crème de
  cacao
2 oz. cream of coconut
Crushed ice
Coconut shavings

Big Old Fashioned; blend
and pour over crushed ice.
Sprinkle coconut shavings
(optional).

PAINTER'S
PALETTE

1 oz. vodka
1 oz. green crème de
  menthe
1/2 oz. Kahlua
1/2 oz. white crème de
  cacao
1/2 oz. cherry brandy
1 tbsp. grenadine

Old Fashioned; pour gently
over ice, stir slowly. Add
red and green cherries.

PEACH PIT

2 oz. peach brandy
1 oz. vodka
1/2 oz. amaretto
1 tsp. lemon juice

Old Fashioned; shake with
ice, strain over ice.

PERVERTED TOMMY

2 oz. gin
1/2 oz. dry vermouth
2 dashes Angostura
  bitters
Dash orange bitters
2 oz. each grapefruit and
  orange juice
1 tbsp. lemon juice

Old Fashioned; shake with
ice, strain over ice.

PIRATE'S COVE

1 1/2 oz. dark rum
1 1/2 oz. light rum
1/2 oz. gold rum
3 oz. cream of coconut
2 oz. pineapple juice
1 oz. crushed ice

Goblet; blend at high
speed, pour.

POLEAXE

1/2 oz. bourbon
1/2 oz. scotch
1/2 oz. rye
3 tbsp. grapefruit juice
1 tsp. lemon juice

Highball; shake with ice,
strain over ice.

QUARK

2 oz. dark rum
1 tbsp. white crème de
  menthe
1 tbsp. vanilla extract

Highball; shake with ice,
strain over ice. Add cherry.

QUEER BAIT

1 1/2 oz. dark rum
1 tbsp. grenadine
1 tbsp. lime juice
2 tbsp. pineapple juice

Highball; shake with ice,
strain over ice. Add cherry.

QUICK FIX

2 oz. light rum
1/2 oz. Kahlua
2 tbsp. heavy cream
Cinnamon

Old Fashioned; shake with
ice, strain over ice. Dust
with cinnamon.

RAISINADE

1 1/2 oz. vodka
1 tbsp. light rum
1 oz. prune juice
Lemonade

Collins; pour over ice, fill
with lemonade, stir. Add
cherry.

REIGN OF TERROR

1 1/2 oz. bourbon
1/2 oz. sloe gin
3 dashes Angostura
  bitters

Highball; shake with ice,
strain over ice. Add lemon
twist.

REPTILE'S BREATH

1 oz. Jagermeister
1/2 oz. dry gin
1 egg white

Old Fashioned; shake with
ice, strain over ice.

RESUSCITATOR

1 oz. light rum
1/2 oz. gold rum
1/2 oz. vodka
1 tsp. apricot brandy
2 tbsp. orange juice

Old Fashioned; shake with
ice, strain over ice. Add
cherry.

ROBED
ARISTOCRAT

2 oz. light rum
1/2 oz. white crème de
  cacao
1/2 tsp. melted butter

Highball; pour over ice,
stir in butter.

ROBOT OIL

1 oz. Sambuca
1 oz. melon liqueur
3 dashes bitters

Old Fashioned; shake with ice, strain over ice. Add lemon twist.

RODAN'S NECTAR

1 oz. vodka
1 oz. amaretto
1 tbsp. banana liqueur

Cocktail; shake with ice, strain over ice.

ROGUE COCKTAIL

1 oz. gin
1 oz. vodka
1/2 oz. dry vermouth
1 crushed cocktail onion

Highball; shake with ice, strain over ice. Add lemon twist.

ROME SPECIAL

No wonder Rome wasn't built in a day.

1 oz. dark rum
1/2 oz. Galliano
1/2 oz. amaretto
2 tbsp. sloe gin

Old Fashioned; shake with ice, strain over ice.

RULER'S COCKTAIL

also called RULER'S SPECIAL

2 oz. cognac
1/2 oz. sweet vermouth
1 egg

Snifter; shake with ice, strain over ice. Add lemon slice.

RUST

Corrosion from within.

1 1/2 oz. whiskey
1/2 oz. white crème de cacao

Cocktail; shake with ice, strain. Chill.

SANTA'S HELPER

1 1/2 oz. cherry or blackberry brandy
1 1/2 oz. peppermint schnapps

Highball; pour over ice, stir gently.

SAP

1 oz. bourbon
1 oz. dark rum
2 tbsp. dark crème de cacao
2 tbsp. maple syrup

Old Fashioned; shake with ice, strain over ice.

SEA SLUG

1 oz. light rum
1 oz. peach schnapps
1/2 oz. vodka
1 tbsp. pineapple juice
Pinch of salt

Highball; shake with ice,
strain over ice. Add salt.

SEPTIC FLUID

also called SEPTIC TANK

2 oz. Bailey's Irish Cream
1 oz. green crème de
menthe
2 tbsp. dark rum

Highball; shake with ice,
strain.

SIMON'S BRAIN

see BRAIN HEMORRHAGE

SINBAD'S 7

3/4 oz. vodka
3/4 oz. gin
1/2 oz. triple sec
1/2 oz. light rum
1/2 oz. dark rum
2 tbsp. green Chartreuse
2 tbsp. whiskey
Orange juice

Goblet; pour over ice, fill
with orange juice, stir.
Add variety of fruits.

SINK OR SWIM

1 1/2 oz. brandy
2 tsp. sweet vermouth
2 dashes Angostura
bitters

Old Fashioned; shake with
ice, strain over ice. Add
lime slice.

SLIMEBALL

1 1/2 oz. Bailey's Irish
Cream
1 1/2 oz. green crème
de menthe
1 tbsp. heavy cream
2 drops lime juice

Cocktail; pour, stir, chill.

SOF

*also called SOLDIER OF
FORTUNE*

2 oz. Irish whiskey
1/2 oz. bourbon
1 egg yolk
2 tsp. lemon juice
2 tsp. grenadine

Old Fashioned; shake with
ice, strain over ice. Add
olive.

TALISMAN

1 1/2 oz. bourbon
1 tbsp. green or yellow
Chartreuse
1 tsp. crème de noyaux

Cocktail; pour over ice,
stir.

TANGO IN BOLIVIA

1 1/2 tequila
2 tsp. white crème de cacao
2 tsp. sloe gin
1 tsp. orange juice
2 drops curaçao
2 drops yellow Chartreuse

Old Fashioned; shake with ice, strain over ice. Add cherry.

TARPON

Robin's favorite fishing drink.

2 tbsp. bourbon
2 tbsp. triple sec
3 oz. orange juice
1 tsp. sugar syrup
Club soda

Highball; shake with ice, strain over ice, fill with soda. Pineapple slice garnish.

TENDER MERCIES

1 1/2 oz. gin
1 tbsp. apple brandy
1 tbsp. apricot brandy
2 drops lemon juice
2 drops lime juice

Old Fashioned; shake with ice, strain over ice.

THUNDER LOVER

Lisa's favorite!

2 oz. dark rum
1 oz. gold rum
2 oz. cream of coconut
1 tbsp. 151-proof rum

Goblet; shake with ice, strain over ice.

TIGER'S MILK

1 oz. Jamaican rum
1 oz. brandy
3 tsp. sugar syrup
3 oz. heavy cream

Big Old Fashioned; shake with ice, strain over ice.

ULCER

Make sure your health insurance is current.

1/2 oz. vodka
1/2 oz. tequila
1/2 oz. dry gin
2 oz. grapefruit juice
1 oz. lemon juice

Old Fashioned; shake with ice, strain over ice.

UNDERTAKER

1 oz. vodka
3/4 oz. gin
1 oz. light cream
1 tsp. Bailey's Irish
  Cream

Highball; shake with ice,
strain.

UP IN SMOKE

2 oz. cognac
1/2 oz. port wine
1 tbsp. lime juice
1 tsp. lemon juice

Old Fashioned; pour over
ice, stir.

V

2 oz. apricot brandy
1 oz. orange juice
1/2 oz. vodka
1 tbsp. lemon juice
2 dashes orange bitters

Old Fashioned; shake with
ice, strain over ice.

VENGEANCE

1 1/2 oz. tequila
1 oz. sloe gin
1/2 oz. whiskey
1 oz. lemon juice

Old Fashioned; shake with
ice, strain over ice. Add
lemon twist.

VORPAL WOUND

1 3/4 oz. tequila
1 oz. brandy
1 tbsp. curaçao
1 oz. grapefruit juice

Old Fashioned; shake with
ice, strain over ice.

WELTS

1 1/2 oz. blackberry
  brandy
1 oz. light rum
1/2 oz. lemon soda

Old Fashioned; pour over
ice, stir.

WITCHES' BREW

see COVEN OF WITCHES

WITCHING HOUR

2 oz. vodka
1/2 oz. Jagermeister
1/2 oz. triple sec
1 tbsp. sweet vermouth

Old Fashioned; shake with
ice, strain over ice.

ZERO HOUR IN THE CATSKILLS

Sometimes a little gamble pays off.

2 oz. Jamaican rum
1/2 oz. lemon-flavored
  vodka
1/2 oz. chocolate syrup
1 tbsp. cherry syrup
1 tsp. brown sugar

Collins; pour over ice, stir. Cherry garnish.

ZORRO

also called CHOCOLATE ZORRO

1 oz. Tia Maria
1/2 oz. cherry brandy
1 tbsp. chocolate syrup

Cocktail; shake with ice, strain. Chill.

Granted, Southern California is not the first place that comes to mind when thinking of sub-zero temperatures or icy weather—although Northern California can provide you with a double dose of those conditions. But botch a few big auditions or have a particularly bad day for a plethora of reasons (something residents of Los Angeles and neighboring communities seem to experience quite often) and there's nothing better than a hot, tasty beverage—usually filled with a healthy dose of alcohol—to take the cold sting out of your day.

Almost always, with the exception of a few "tea" drinks, these concoctions are served in coffee mugs (Hot Mugs) or hot chocolate goblets. Garnishes and accoutrements do vary, but in most cases it's up to the creator—or the customer. Just to be safe, I'd keep on hand chocolate shavings, cinnamon, colored or chocolate sprinkles, mini-marshmallows, and, of course, the ever-popular whipped cream. Try these drinks alone or, if you're bold and brazen, in haphazard combinations. Whichever way you choose, they should be pleasing to both the eyes and the palate. (Well, *some* palates anyway!) However, for some drinks, specific garnishes are listed.

ALBINO MELTDOWN

1 oz. Sambuca
1/2 oz. light rum
1/4 oz. sweet vermouth
Coffee
Milk

Hot Mug; half-fill with hot coffee, add other ingredients, fill with milk, stir. Garnish to taste.

ATHLETE'S WARM-UP

1 oz. vodka
1/2 oz. Galliano
1 tbsp. chocolate syrup
Coffee or hot chocolate
  (if hot chocolate, leave
  out chocolate syrup)

Hot Mug; pour ingredients, fill with hot coffee, stir. Whipped cream garnish only.

APPLESEED JOHNNY'S HOME BREW

A favorite of all New Yorkers.

1 1/2 oz. whiskey
1/2 oz. apple schnapps
1 tbsp. vanilla syrup
1 tsp. cinnamon
1 tsp. brown sugar
Coffee

Hot Mug; pour ingredients, fill with hot coffee, stir. Do not garnish.

AUNT JEMIMA'S BREAKFAST SPECIAL

Who needs pancakes and waffles?

1 1/2 oz. whiskey
1 oz. Tia Maria
1 tsp. sugar syrup
1 egg yolk
Coffee

Hot Mug; mix egg yolk and other ingredients, stir vigorously, strain, fill with hot coffee. Garnish to taste.

ARTS AND CRAFTS

No popsicle sticks here.

2 oz. Kahlua
1 oz. cherry brandy
Coffee

Hot Mug; pour ingredients, fill with coffee, stir. Garnish to taste.

BULGARIAN SLUDGE

And you thought L.A. was bad after a rainstorm.

2 oz. tequila
1 tbsp. 151-proof rum
1 tbsp. cherry syrup
Hot chocolate

Hot Mug; half-fill with hot chocolate, stir in ingredients. Fill with whipped cream.

CHOCOLATE ANEURISM

Willy Wonka's worst nightmare.

1 1/2 oz. dark crème de cacao
1 oz. light crème de cacao
2 tbsp. vanilla
1 tsp. brown sugar
Dash peppermint schnapps
Hot chocolate

Hot Mug; pour 3/4 full with hot chocolate, stir in ingredients. Garnish to taste.

CIDER-HATER

1 1/2 oz. pear or peach brandy
1 tbsp. spiced rum
1 squeeze of fresh lemon
Hot tea

Teacup; pour 3/4 full with tea, add ingredients, stir.

For RUSSIAN CIDER-HATER, serve in Collins glass.

COFFEE OF THE DAMNED

Even zombies avoid this elixir.

1 oz. scotch
1 oz. brandy
1/2 oz. tequila
1 tbsp. sugar syrup
1 tsp. shredded lemon pulp
Coffee

Hot Mug; pour ingredients, fill with hot coffee, stir. Whipped cream garnish. Float lemon pulp.

COMPTON COFFEE

2 oz. vodka
1/2 oz. port wine
1/2 oz. peppermint schnapps
Coffee

Hot Mug; add ingredients, fill with hot coffee, stir. Serve black without garnish.

CURSED WATER

More effective than Holy Water on vampires!

1 oz. 151-proof rum
1/2 oz. gin
1/4 oz. peach schnapps
1 tbsp. honey
Hot tea

Hot Mug; pour 3/4 full with tea, add ingredients, stir gently. Add lemon slice.

DOGWATER FLUID

Stops all brain functions.

2 tbsp. Everclear or grain
  alcohol
1 tsp. lemon juice
1 to 2 pinches salt
Coffee

Hot Mug; fill with hot coffee, add ingredients, stir.

EVIL-EYED JOSEPHINE

Not a woman you want to cross.

1 1/2 oz. black cherry
  brandy
1/2 oz. Kahlua
1/2 oz. pineapple juice
1 tbsp. dark crème de
  cacao
Coffee

Hot Mug; half-fill with hot coffee, stir in ingredients. Whipped cream garnish.

FRENCH KILLER

1 oz. Frangelico
1/2 oz. crème de noyaux
2 tbsp. cream
Coffee

Hot Mug; pour liqueurs, fill with hot coffee, add cream, stir. Garnish only with whipped cream.

FUGARI

Italian for "Ugggh!"

1 oz. Campari
1 tsp. lime juice
2 to 3 chocolate morsels
  (chips)
Hot tea

Teacup; pour 3/4 full with tea, add ingredients, do not stir. Garnish with mint sprig.

GALWAY

Screenwriter Sean's favorite potion.

1 1/2 oz. Irish whiskey
1/2 oz. Frangelico
1 tbsp. amaretto
1 tbsp. Kahlua
Coffee

Hot Mug; add ingredients, fill with hot coffee, stir. Garnish with whipped cream.

HEADMASTER'S BREW

Private school, anyone?

1 oz. scotch
2 tbsp. brandy
1 tsp. cinnamon
  schnapps
1 tsp. cream
Coffee

Hot Mug; add ingredients, fill with hot coffee, stir. Add cream, stir. Garnish to taste.

HOT ANACONDA

Squeezes the life right out of you.

2 oz. dark rum
1/2 oz. Kahlua
1/2 oz. Bailey's Irish
  Cream
1/2 oz. cream
Hot chocolate

Hot Mug; pour ingredients, fill with hot chocolate. Garnish to taste.

HOT BANANA SMOKER

Because it's a jungle out there!

1 1/2 oz. vodka
1 oz. light crème de
  cacao
1 oz. banana brandy
2 tbsp. cream of coconut
1 peeled banana
Coffee

Hot Mug; pour ingredients, fill with hot coffee, stir. Add banana. Garnish with whipped cream.

HOT CAMBODIAN SLUSH

1 oz. tequila
1 oz. gin
1/2 oz. coffee liqueur
Coffee

Hot Mug; pour 3/4 full with hot coffee, add ingredients, stir. No garnish.

HOT JAMAICAN RUM-OFF

Ya' mon, we be jammin'.

2 oz. Jamaican rum
1 oz. Malibu rum
1 tbsp. 151-proof rum
Coffee

Hot Mug; pour rums, fill with hot coffee, stir. Garnish to taste. Play Bob Marley's CD.

HOT SAUCE

You don't want to put this on your taco.

1 oz. cherry brandy
1 oz. cinnamon schnapps
1 tsp. Tabasco sauce
1 tsp. cinnamon
Coffee

Hot Mug; half-fill with hot coffee, add ingredients, stir. Whipped cream garnish. Dust with cinnamon.

HULKING INFORMANT

This one doesn't need the Witness Protection Program.

2 oz. scotch
1/2 oz. Southern Comfort
1/2 oz. Drambuie
1 tbsp. peach schnapps
Hot chocolate

Hot Mug; pour ingredients, fill with hot chocolate. Mini-marshmallow garnish.

ICE-MELTING CRYOFLUID

1 oz. vodka
1 tbsp. peppermint
  schnapps
1 tbsp. lemon or lime
  juice
1 Pinch salt
Hot tea

Beer Mug; pour ingredients, fill with tea, stir. Add salt. Float ice cube.

IRISH COFFEE

1 to 2 oz. Irish whiskey
Coffee

Hot Mug; pour Irish whiskey. Fill with hot coffee, stir. Whipped cream garnish.

ISLAND HEATWAVE

2 oz. spiced rum
1/2 oz. Galliano
1 tbsp. banana liqueur
Milk
Coffee

Hot Mug; half-fill with hot coffee, add ingredients, stir. Fill with milk. Garnish to taste.

IVORY COAST COFFEE

1 1/2 oz. scotch
2 tbsp. dark crème de
  cacao
2 tbsp. brandy
1 tsp. crème de noyaux
Coffee

Hot Mug; add ingredients, fill with hot coffee, stir gently. No garnish.

JAMBALAYAN COFFEE

You won't find any crawfish here!

1 oz. apricot brandy
1/2 oz. amaretto
2 tbsp. Kahlua
Coffee

Hot Mug; pour 3/4 full with hot coffee, add ingredients, stir. Garnish to taste.

JENSEN

For fans of the Intercepter.

2 oz. gin
1 tsp. scotch
Hot tea

Teacup; add ingredients, fill with tea, stir.

JORDANIAN COOLER

1 oz. gin
1/2 oz. dry vermouth
1 tbsp. sugar syrup
1 tbsp. crushed cherries
Coffee

Hot Mug; pour 3/4 full with hot coffee, add ingredients, stir. Add cherries. Garnish to taste.

KALIFORNIA SUNSET

The perfect ending to a 6.8 day.

2 oz. vodka
1 oz. Jack Daniels
1 tsp. brandy
1 tsp. honey
Coffee

Hot Mug; half-fill with hot coffee, add ingredients, do not stir. Garnish to taste.

KILLER'S COFFEE

A favorite of the boys in San Quentin.

1 1/2 oz. whiskey
1 oz. sweet vermouth
1 tbsp. prune juice
1 tsp. brown sugar
Coffee

Hot Mug; add ingredients, fill with hot coffee, stir gently. No garnish.

LOVER'S DELUSION COFFEE

3 oz. Kahlua
2 oz. amaretto
1 oz. Tia Maria
1 oz. Bailey's Irish Cream
1 oz. brandy
Pot of coffee

Hot Mugs; brew coffee, add ingredients, stir vigorously. Pour and garnish to taste. (Serves 2)

MOURNING BLEND

Not *something to wake up to!*

2 oz. scotch
2 tbsp. apple brandy
1 tbsp. dark rum
1 tsp. 151-proof rum
Coffee

Hot Mug; add ingredients, fill with hot coffee, stir. Float 151-proof rum. Garnish to taste.

MYSTERY STEW

1 1/2 oz. Canadian whiskey
1 oz. Kahlua
1 tbsp. light crème de cacao
Coffee and hot chocolate

Hot Mug; add ingredients, fill with equal parts coffee and hot chocolate, stir. Garnish to taste.

NATURALIST'S COFFEE

Real big with the camping crowd.

1/2 oz. whiskey
1/2 oz. Bailey's Irish Cream
2 to 3 drops Everclear or grain alcohol
Coffee

Hot Mug; pour ingredients, fill with hot coffee, stir. Add grain alcohol. No garnish.

NAYSAYER'S TEA

1 tbsp. vodka
1 tbsp. sweet vermouth
1 tsp. port wine
Hot tea

Hot Mug; pour 3/4 full
with tea, add ingredients,
stir gently. Add thin
lemon slice.

NOCTURNAL ASSURANCE

I dare you to sleep!

1 oz. vodka
1 tbsp. peppermint
  schnapps
1 tsp. 151-proof rum
Espresso

Hot Mug; pour 3/4 full
with espresso, add ingredients, stir. Float 151-proof
rum. No garnish.

NUTRITIONIST'S COFFEE

This can't *be healthy.*

1 oz. Kahlua
1 oz. low- or nonfat milk
1/2 oz. amaretto
2 tbsp. protein powder
3 egg whites
1 egg yolk
Coffee

Goblet; blend ingredients,
strain into goblet, fill with
hot coffee, stir. No garnish.

ORGAN WARMER

*Great for frost-bitten
egos, too.*

1 1/2 oz. cognac
1 oz. light crème de
  cacao
Hot chocolate

Hot Mug; add ingredients,
fill with hot chocolate,
stir. Garnish to taste.

PACIFIC COFFEE

2 oz. dark rum
1 tbsp. whiskey
1 tbsp. honey
1 tsp. vanilla syrup
1 to 2 pinches brown
  sugar
1 to 2 drops lemon juice
Coffee

Hot Mug; pour ingredients,
fill with hot coffee, add
honey, stir. No garnish.

POLAR BEAR PISS

*Melts everything from ice
to icebergs.*

1 oz. scotch
1 oz. whiskey
1 oz. dark rum
1 tbsp. cherry brandy
3 tbsp. milk
1 tsp. lemon syrup
Coffee

Hot Mug; pour ingredients,
add hot coffee to 3/4 full,
stir. Add milk, stir. Drizzle
lemon syrup. Garnish to
taste.

PRIMATE'S CHOICE

This is all they serve at the San Diego Zoo.

1/2 oz. tequila
1/2 oz. apricot or pear
  brandy
1 tbsp. vanilla syrup
1 tsp. dark crème de
  cacao
Hot chocolate

Hot Mug; pour ingredients, fill with hot chocolate, stir. Garnish to taste.

ROSENBERRY BREW

A big hit with all the literary agents.

1 oz. lemon-flavored
  vodka
1/2 oz. crème de noyaux
1/2 oz. cherry brandy
1 tbsp. strawberry syrup
1/2 tsp. brown sugar
Coffee

Hot Mug; pour ingredients, fill with hot coffee, stir. Trickle syrup. Dust brown sugar. Garnish to taste.

SALAMANDER TEA

1/2 to 3/4 oz. sweet
  vermouth
2 tbsp. port wine
1 tbsp. dark rum
1 tsp. dark crème de
  cacao
1 tsp. honey
Hot tea

Hot Mug; pour ingredients, fill with tea, stir gently. Add honey.

STETSON

For the cowboy in all of us.

1 1/2 oz. Jack Daniels
1/2 oz. amaretto
1 tbsp. maple syrup
Coffee

Hot Mug; pour 3/4 full with hot coffee, add ingredients, stir. Garnish to taste.

SUNDOWN OVER MALIBU

You need not be a millionaire to enjoy this, but it helps.

1 1/2 oz. champagne
  (preferably Dom
  Perignon or Bollinger)
1 tsp. cognac
Hot tea

Snifter; pour 3/4 full with hot tea, add ingredients, stir.

TAMARAC CHOCOLATE NOOSE

Another Catskill specialty.

1 oz. brandy
1 oz. Bailey's Irish Cream
2 tbsp. white crème de menthe
1 tbsp. butterscotch syrup
Hot chocolate

Hot Mug; pour ingredients, fill with hot chocolate, stir gently. Garnish to taste.

TRIALL COFFEE

A special at the Bluebird House.

1 1/2 oz. Jamaican rum
1/2 oz. white crème de cacao
1 tbsp. Frangelico
Coffee

Hot Mug; pour ingredients, fill with hot coffee, stir. Garnish to taste.

WHITE CHOCOLATE ECSTASY

2 oz. dark crème de cacao
1 oz. white crème de cacao
1 oz. green crème de menthe
Milk
Coffee

Hot Mug; pour ingredients, add hot coffee to 3/4 full, fill with milk, stir. Garnish to taste.

DRINKS FOR THE DESIGNATED DRIVER

Alas, there has to be *one* responsible member in your drinking party. At least, I hope that's the case. So, to appeal to the responsible drinker, I've assembled this final category—although it should be noted that non-alcoholic elixirs number well into the millions. Just about any combination of juices, syrups, sodas, and other non-fermented ingredients can be combined, producing an endless selection of tastes, enough to suit, or offend, any palate on earth.

Use your imagination—if you dare—and see what works best for you, or for the non-drinker you're serving. But in the meanwhile, while you're brainstorming, I've listed a few of my favorites.

ARNOLD PALMER

Golfer Sande's favorite post-round cool-down.

Equal parts of ice tea and lemonade, served in a tall glass with plenty of ice.
This drink works equally well—if not better—with flavored teas and/or pink lemonade.

COLA

If you can't figure this one out, call 1-800-IMA-PUTZ! (Any clean glass will work.)

CRANBERRY BOMBER

4 oz. cranberry juice
1/2 oz. orange juice
2 tbsp. grenadine
1 tsp. honey
Cola

Collins; pour over ice, fill with cola, stir. Add honey. Lemon garnish.

DEVIL'S JUICE

Bring breath mints.

3 oz. cranberry (or
  cranapple) juice
3 oz. tomato juice
1 tsp. Tabasco sauce
1 tsp. lemon juice
2 dashes black pepper
Dash salt

Collins; pour over ice, stir.
Lemon and parsley garnish.

EVIL PRINCESS

1 oz. grenadine
1 oz. lemon juice
1/2 fresh lime
7-Up or Sprite

Collins; pour over ice, fill
with 7-Up, stir. Squeeze
lime juice. Cherry garnish.

GLASER JUICE

2 oz. pineapple juice
2 oz. white grape juice
1 oz. apple juice
2 tbsp. vanilla syrup
1 tbsp. lemon juice

Collins; pour over ice, stir.
Lime garnish.

HEALTH NUT'S RECOVERY SHAKE

*Personal trainer Lisa
swears by these.*

4 oz. low- or nonfat milk
2 oz. non-alcoholic
  egg-nog (you may
  substitute 2 oz.
  Egg-Beaters for egg-nog)
3 oz. protein powder
2 tbsp. wheat germ
2 tbsp. chocolate syrup

Goblet; blend at high
speed, strain.

ICE WATER

A no-brainer.

Very similar to that tough-
to-mix concoction called
COLA. (Use a clean glass.)

JUICE

*Nature's own homemade
beverage.*

Take your pick, pour it
over ice, and go for it.

PROTEIN REPLENISHER

For drunks and athletes alike.

2 oz. grapefruit juice
2 oz. carrot or celery juice
2 oz. low-fat milk
2 egg whites
1 tbsp. honey
1 tsp. lime juice

Beer Mug; blend at high speed, pour. Strawberry garnish.

SAMURAI COOLER

3 oz. apple juice
1 oz. pineapple juice
1 oz. orange juice
1 tsp. ginseng extract
Ginger ale

Collins; pour over ice, fill with ginger ale, stir. Float ginseng extract. Cherry garnish.

SODA

Very similar to COLA, without the color or sugar. I think you can figure it out.

VOLCANO COOLER

2 scoops rainbow sherbet
4 oz. milk
2 oz. orange juice
1 oz. club soda
1 tbsp. lemon juice

Goblet; blend ingredients, pour. Pineapple slice garnish.

It seems fitting that this chapter appears at the end of the book, since the aftermath of an evening spent overindulging your affinity for cocktails usually culminates with a visit from the unwanted guest everyone loves to hate: the hangover.

But fear not, my liquor-drinking friends, for just as I have provided you with a plethora of recipes, I shall also reveal a few of my favorite cures—mind you, ones that actually work—to return your body and mind to its pre-multiple-cocktail state of normalcy. However, if you felt like chopped liver and your mind was altered *before* your pour 'em and slam 'em binge, I'm afraid there's nothing I can do for you.

DRINKS:

BREAKFAST IN A GLASS

Rocky's favorite ... sort of!

3 eggs
4 oz. tomato juice
4 oz. orange juice
1 tsp. lemon juice
2 to 3 dashes Tabasco
  sauce

Blend at high speed until frothy; serve.

Crushed ice can also be added to blender for a "frozen" version.

FIVE AND FIVE

Not for the cholesterol-conscious!

5 oz. tomato juice
5 eggs
1 tbsp. Worcestershire
  sauce

Blend at high speed; serve.

HAIR OF THE DOG

6 oz. prune juice
2 oz. orange juice
1 oz. milk (or 1/2 oz. heavy cream)

Pour over ice, stir; serve.

HANGOVER ANNIHILATOR

1 egg yolk
8 oz. tomato or V-8 juice
Juice of 1 lemon
Pinch of salt

Stir briskly (enough to mix the yolk); serve.

ORANGE REPLENISHER

5 oz. fresh carrot juice
5 oz. orange juice
1 tbsp. honey
1 tsp. lemon juice

Stir; strain over ice.

SUNRISE FOR THE DAMNED

8 oz. orange juice
1 oz. club soda or ginger ale
2 tbsp. honey
1 egg yolk
1 tsp. brown sugar

Shake with ice (or blend with ice); strain; serve.

FOODS:

DRY TOAST

It's lame and it doesn't always work, but you don't have to be Julia Child to prepare it.

GARBAGE PAIL OMELET

Keep Tums or Pepto-Bismol nearby.

4 eggs (or egg whites for you health nuts out there)
Anything in the 'fridge that doesn't smell like it's spoiled
1 dollop butter or margarine

Mix; cook; serve.

HANGOVER OMELET

Sande, this is my gift to you.

4 eggs
2 to 3 oz. chopped turkey or sliced turkey breast
2 to 3 oz. chopped roast beef or sliced roast beef
1/8 cup chopped green and red bell peppers
1/8 cup chopped onions
1 tsp. crushed garlic
1 dollop butter or margarine
Swiss cheese—as much as you can take!

Mix all except cheese; pour into a skillet; add cheese; cook; eat.

Truthfully, I don't know if it'll help, but it tastes really good.

7 eggs (use only 3 yolks)
4 oz. chopped salami
   (preferably reduced fat,
   low-sodium or smoked)
1 dollop butter or mar-
   garine

Mix all "scrambled egg style" and serve. (Serves 2)

Mr. Sandman, bring me a dream...

Mix one mattress—or otherwise comfortable place—with the affected individual(s). Add quiet and darkness; do not stir for at least 7 hours. Repeat if necessary.

BAR TRIVIA

Every now and then, customers will want to bet the bartender a drink that they can't be stumped. Here are a few trivia questions you should win on every time.

THE QUESTIONS:
1. On "Gilligan's Island," what was the Skipper's real name? (Not the actor's name, the character's name.)
2. In what year, since the start of production, did Chevrolet build the fewest number of Corvettes?
3. What's the only animal in the world that carries a badge?
4. What is significant about the title of the James Bond film "Goldeneye"?

THE ANSWERS:
1. Jonas Grumby.
2. 1983. Chevrolet built zero. They were barren between 1982 and 1984, introducing a new body style in '84.
3. A police horse.
4. It was the name of Ian Fleming's house in Jamaica.

A

B

M

200